SPLIT

A CHILD, A PRIEST, AND THE CATHOLIC CHURCH

SPLIT

A CHILD,
A PRIEST, AND
THE CATHOLIC CHURCH

MARY DISPENZA

MOON DAY PRESS

Cover and Interior Design: Kathryn Campbell
Cover Photo by Mary Dispenza

SPLIT: A Child, a Priest, and the Catholic Church
Print Edition ISBN 978-0-9896563-2-0
MOBI Edition ISBN 978-0-9896563-3-7
EPUB Edition ISBN 978-0-9896563-4-4

Library of Congress Control Number: 2014913616

Printed in the United States of America by IngramSpark
Published in the United States of America by
Moon Day Press, Bellevue, Washington

For Mary Ann

Foreword

The sexual abuse crisis in the Catholic Church is so long running, and so widespread, that it has come to be known by the raw numbers that catalogue the devastation:

> Thousands of victims.
>
> More than 1,000 priests deemed "credibly accused," by the church's definition.
>
> Five hundred American priests jailed on criminal convictions.
>
> $3 billion paid to compensate victims worldwide.

As the scandal moved from city to city, and then nation to nation, it became all too easy to forget that, in every act of abuse, a boy or girl was physically, emotionally, and spiritually harmed and that the wounds they suffer are deep and long lasting. Violated in childhood, these children carry the pain into adulthood, where it can affect their lives in myriad ways. From anxiety and self-doubt to deep depression and despair, the aftereffects of childhood sexual trauma are real.

Fortunately, since the beginning of the crisis, we have benefitted from the brave and honest testimony of victims, told in depositions, court proceedings, media accounts, and memoirs, to keep us grounded in the truth of the crimes that reside at its core. In Mary Dispenza's *SPLIT*, we now have a most compelling example of this truth telling, executed with unique emotional clarity and generosity. Her memoir of the betrayal that is clergy abuse—and her own recovery—offers both a mature perspective and raw honesty. It also gives us hope.

In these pages we meet the little girl in blonde pigtails who loved the life she knew, which was full of family, church, and community. We follow her into the Los Angeles neighborhood where she grew up, to the parish where she attended mass and to the school where she adored everyone, including the lunch ladies in their hairnets.

The end of Mary's innocence came when she was seven years old and she wandered into the nearly empty nearby school auditorium for a special treat—a movie displayed in the flickering light of an old-fashioned film projector. In the darkness, a man she knew as "Father" committed a crime that lasted maybe fifteen minutes, maybe a lifetime. From that moment on, the girl who played Annie Oakley in the yard was subject to the kind of shame, guilt, confusion, and grief that no seven-year-old can bear. As a result, her adolescence and early adulthood were marked by far more than the usual pain and tumult. Before she was fully adult, she became a nun, embracing a life of service, restraint, and humility.

Wise and generous, Mary takes us into the world she found as a sister, crediting the women she met there with quite possibly saving her life. "They loved me into aspects of myself that I cherish today," she explains, even as she notes the sacrifices she was required to make and the losses that she accepted. All the while, the sexual abuse she suffered as a girl frequently forced her into a state of dissociation, robbing her of genuine emotional experiences. Often lost to herself and others, she felt like a miner trapped in a collapsed tunnel, feeling the dark isolation and never knowing if rescue would come.

In Mary's quest to rescue herself, she has to face the reality of the all-too-common abuse of power inside the church bureaucracy and the institution's preference for self-preservation—and face saving—over the safety and welfare of its most vulnerable members. However, as *SPLIT* shows, the human spirit is often more resilient than we can imagine. This thrilling truth lies at the inspiring heart of this wonderful work and it comes with many searing, as well as delightful, surprises. The beauty in *SPLIT* is that it is also a story of someone who is unbowed, undaunted, and unbroken. If you have ever felt the discouragement that so many feel as they reflect on the Catholic crisis, you will find the antidote here.

—Michael D' Antonio

Pulitzer Prize-winning journalist, author of *Mortal Sins: Sex, Crime and the Era of Catholic Scandal* and a 2014 recipient of an Edgar Award for Best Crime Nominee

Introduction

He was a priest—a man sent by God. That was what I knew about him. I called him Father. He seemed to like me because he held my hand and walked with me around the schoolyard.

I was seven years old. I must have trusted him, to sit on his lap.

Rape makes years fade together. Memories stand frozen.

Sixty-seven years later and still I do not know him; I only know of him. He is a Catholic priest, but he is no angel. He is a serial pedophile in the diocese of Los Angeles, the City of the Angels, and he hurt me. Angels don't rape children, don't poison them with memories that will haunt them for many years, perhaps all their lives.

This is a story about putting the invisible pieces of spirituality and sexuality back together and learning to live without shame.

Little Mary

CIRCLE OF SHAME

*He was awake a long time before he
remembered that his heart was broken.*

—Ernest Hemingway, *For Whom the Bell Tolls*

THE FLASHBACK CAME over me like a piece of somebody else's
film spliced into my personal reel. In a blink, it was 1947 again
and I was back at St. Alphonsus School in East Los Angeles—
the place where the priest raped me, then abandoned me, again,
and again, and again. Back in the place where I sentenced myself
to a prison of shame.

I may have been forty-nine on the outside that day, but inside,
I was a seven-year-old child. I remember the box lunches and
the notebook I was handed to record any personal notes from
the day's lectures and discussions on the *Sexual Misconduct on
the Part of Clergy.*

I don't remember precisely what unleashed this flashback,
whether it was a story someone shared, a group activity, or perhaps the things no one said out loud but that showed behind
the eyes. The kinds of things you only see because it takes one to
know one. The vivid memory left my hands clammy. Confused,
I only knew that something inside of me wanted out and it had
been hidden for decades.

Earlier that day I sank into one of the hard folding chairs
at a long table and stared at the title of the notebook. My eyes
locked on to the words: *Sexual Misconduct.* As I waited for the
workshop to begin, I paged idly through my notebook, saying

hello to colleagues as they entered.

I was both uneasy and excited to be in this room. It was 1989 and I was new to my job as director of the Pastoral Life Services for the Catholic Archdiocese of Seattle. After greeting several new arrivals, I became aware of how little I knew about them and how much I had to learn about this position. This workshop—required of all Chancery Department heads and diocesan leaders—gave me the opportunity to know at least some of them better, but it wasn't a topic I looked forward to delving into.

The appointment to my new position came from Archbishops Raymond Hunthausen and Thomas Murphy of the Archdiocese of Seattle and was an honor. A nun for fifteen years, a teacher and principal in Catholic schools for thirty years, I was ready for this change in ministry. I was not ready for where the workshop would lead me.

The words I heard in the workshop that day rattled my life-long respect for priests with terms like *child abuse*, *pedophilia*, and *molestation*. The words hit hard on my chest, penetrated to my heart. The room was spinning. I was spinning.

The words cracked me open, bit by bit, like tiny hammers on a shell. My body was breaking apart. But why? This wasn't about me. Was it?

Chip, chip, crack, crack—the information being presented was letting in enough light that my soul wanted more. And then it was as if I were a baby chick, pecking to come free. I had been safe in my shell. In fact, I hadn't even known I was huddled in a shell at all. Now some forgotten part of myself was twisting, turning, trying to break out of this hard exterior I had created. Who was this chick?

Memories returned, the whirring stopped, as words from the workshop presenter took over. "If you have suspicions about a priest and child abuse, you must report this to the authorities. That is your responsibility." The words continued to chisel away at me.

My heart raced while I drove away from the workshop. I was shaken to the core. I didn't understand why here, why now, I was coming face-to-face with the buried truth that a priest had sexually abused me.

Once I was back home, not being one to sit still, I immediately went to the phone and dialed directory assistance for Los Angeles, scribbled the phone number I was given on a scrap of paper, and dialed the number of the man I had kept locked out of my awareness since I was seven years old.

"Hello. . ." a priest answered. It was not the priest I'd asked for. "Just a moment. I will get him."

I heard his footsteps coming nearer and nearer to the receiver, but that was as far as I could take it on that day. I hung up in a panic. That night, I made another call. This one was to the presenters of that day's workshop, The Sexual Misconduct of Clergy.

The spinning feeling in the workshop and the spinning dial of my old phone brought a familiar discomfort, but that call changed the course of my life. Sister Francine answered, and I gave her a brief overview of why I had called her, in my very halting, terrified voice. Her response was immediate and definitive. "I will need to report this." The word *this* embodied the shame I felt when I said to her, "I was molested by a priest when I was seven." Shame was always lurking around in me with issues of sexuality. Sister Francine sensed the shame and fear in me. "You know, Mary, it wasn't your fault. You are brave to tell me." Wise and experienced, she encouraged me to follow up with her. "Please come and join a circle of other women who were molested by priests." This was an invitation I never dreamed I'd receive.

Despite the strangeness of it, something compelled me to accept. Perhaps it was that little chick again.

Sleep that night was a foggy sort of rest—in and out of past and present, not quite sure of either. I waited for sunrise with my mind racing, struggling to put these pieces together.

Not more than a week passed when I got to the circle of other women at Therapy and Renewal Associates (TARA) for the Archdiocese of Seattle—and there I spun some more, listening for the first time to stories of other women within the Catholic Church who had been abused by priests. Many of their stories were like mine, except that I was the only woman who had been abused as a child.

The women became my friends and were also loyal, faithful members of the Catholic Church. Some talked about betrayal. One woman had fire in her eyes. I had bewilderment in mine, lost as I was in my attempts to be loyal and critical at the same time, trapped between the glory and the shame of the Catholic Church.

Eight other women told their stories during that hour-long meeting. Over and over again, the tale was how a priest had crossed boundaries, misused his power, abused and left wreckage behind as he went on from parish to parish. I remained silent, having no words to speak.

Abuse had stolen my voice when I was seven years old—a little girl with blond pigtails and a dimple in my left cheek. Mom explained my dimple to me, "Mary, you were shot with an arrow by Cupid in that spot." I loved the thought of that little, soft naked baby with a heart and a bow ready to shoot everyone with his arrow of love.

But then that changed. Everything changed.

Of course I had no way of knowing, then, that the wreckage doesn't always show on the outside. Mine lived within me. Something shut down. Silence, secrecy, and shame became my companions. Childhood priest abuse buried itself in my soul, no feelings, no memory. Gone.

The circle continued to spin, like the film reels of the old movie projector in the school auditorium that awful day. Would the whirring ever stop?

God, make it stop, Little Mary prayed. *Make it stop.*

2

GOOD DAY—BAD DAY

What we call the beginning is often the end
and to make an end is to make a beginning.
The end is where we start.

— T. S. Eliot, *Four Quartets, Little Gidding*

IT WAS AN ORDINARY SCHOOL DAY, just a regular day with reading, writing, learning about God, saying our prayers, lunchtime, playtime, and lots of California sunshine. Mom drove the school bus and did some work in the rectory to make extra money and to swap work for our Catholic school tuition. While she helped with parish business, I fell into his hands.

"Where's Mom?" I asked the lady in the rectory.

"She's over at the school."

She'd be chatting with the lunchroom ladies. I loved those ladies. They had Cupid in their hearts and I knew it—except for Mrs. Horn. I thought her name fit her. She was the lunchroom sergeant who would shake my milk carton to see if I had hidden any canned peas in it. I always did and was always caught and always sent back to my bench to eat my mushy peas. I never gave up trying, and she never gave up shaking my milk carton. I was a smart, clever kid, hiding those hated peas in my milk carton.

I ran across the street from the rectory to the school building, skipped over the cracks in the sidewalk, hopped down the stairs and found Mom with the lunchroom ladies—Mrs. Horn, Mrs. Benjamin, and Mrs. Brennan. All three women were wearing hairnets and blue-green uniform dresses. I adored hairnets and vowed to find one … or steal one … whichever came first. Mom and the ladies were chatting, or maybe gossiping, or maybe eating mushy peas left over from lunch. I was glad somebody might eat them.

Mom ignored me and kept laughing and carrying on. Bored, I opened the door from the lunchroom and peeked into the school auditorium. It was dark inside. Usually it was bright. Although it was on the lower floor of the school building, the tall, many-paned windows let in enough light to take away the darkness. As a second grader, I had never been in the auditorium when it was dark. I had never seen the old drab curtains closed either. The darkness was unusual. I was curious.

That day, rows and rows of light gray folding chairs filled the otherwise empty space. Everything else was the same as usual—the three fat, round posts went down each side of the auditorium to hold up the ceiling, the maroon stage curtain was in place, the old brown speaker boxes hung crookedly on each side of the stage, and the swinging doors, which flung open when you pushed on them, were just as they had been the last time I saw them.

But something was different. A sound I had heard at the start of movies and cartoons caught my attention; the *click, click, click* sound that accompanied the big numbers four, three, two, one before the movie or cartoon started.

Then the sound changed into a whir. I liked that sound. It meant fun, and sometimes, popcorn. I walked down the open center aisle with light gray folding chairs on either side. I felt that possibly, possibly Jesus had parted the sea of chairs for me, just as he did the water for the Israelites. I followed the sound coming from the whirring machine and the small bit of light I saw shining from it.

As I got closer to the machine, I noticed Father. At first I had not seen him in the dark. In his black dress, he disappeared into darkness. He was tall when he was standing, but regular-sized sitting. I liked how he looked, nice and holy in his black dress and white collar. He turned, motioned to me to crawl up on his lap. That's what I did, because I called him Father. I crawled up onto his lap.

Whir, whir, whir, went the projector. I loved the sound of it, *click, click, click*. Being so close was like getting a first-row seat at the baseball game. I watched the film unwind from one reel to the other, delivering a movie right before my eyes. *I'm going to have to tell Mom and Dad and Nickie about this*, I thought. *Nickie will be jealous.* It was magical, until ...

The priest's arm tightened around me and my body tightened with it. Something was changing. I felt trapped. I grew sweaty where his arm held me so tightly. The whirring slowed. The picture began to fade. His legs, which held me gently at first, stiffened. I wanted to say something. My voice wasn't working. Then his other hand slipped under my uniform skirt and he found my panties, and then Father slipped his hand under my panties and he touched me down there. His fingers pushed into me. *What are you doing?* I asked in silence, but I didn't speak a word, couldn't make a sound. His fingers were inside me now. In and out, in and out. I stayed still. It wasn't fun anymore. The light stopped shining, the whirring and clicking sounds of the machine stopped.

Mom, where are you?

Mushy peas. Please pay attention, come get me.

For maybe fifteen minutes, maybe more, time faded along with the picture on the screen. Then Father took my hand in his big hand, like he did in the play yard. He walked me through the parted chairs to the back of the hall. Did he speak? I don't know. I wasn't really there.

Father Rucker walked out of the auditorium and into the sunshine. He did not look back at me. He left me standing in darkness, at the back of the auditorium, alone among the chairs.

I wanted my mommy. I wanted to run to her. I wanted her to throw her arms around me, and kiss me and hold me close to her heart. I wanted my mom to make it all better.

But I felt like I was floating around. Floating around. I didn't understand what had just happened, but I knew it to be a very bad thing and I was so ashamed. There was no way I could reason my way through it, but I sensed that something very bad had taken place and I knew it somehow involved me.

The small bathroom at the back of the auditorium called to me. It seemed so tiny. It was the color of our light brown dog and cold like the air of the freezer when you first put your head into it to see what's there. The faucet knobs, with the *H* and the *C*, looked different that day. The crisscrossed-spoke circles that I used to love to turn one way, then the other, and make the water go splish-splash, had disappeared. I had disappeared.

My small body was shaking. I stretched up to see myself in the mirror. The little girl at the sink and the little girl in the mirror were no longer connected. I began to talk to Jesus and God, because something bad had happened and the fact that I didn't understand it was no comfort to me in my sense of responsibility, my sense of sin. *I love you, God. I love you, Jesus. Bless me God...*

Turning the water on, water splashing over me, I rubbed and rubbed my hands together, washing and washing. I felt smaller and smaller until I disappeared into a little heap on the cold, speckled linoleum floor.

I am in a ball now, curled like a little wet kitten.

It would be some time before someone came and found Little Mary and lifted her up from the bathroom floor.

I'll never know if others came and went that day without noticing Little Mary curled into her trauma, hiding. I myself didn't notice her.

Years later, I returned to this same school as a teacher and then principal. I was there from age twenty-five to thirty-two and still split. I was a Catholic. I was a religious woman, married to Christ and prepared to carry whatever burdens such a life might demand. But the sheer weight of raped Little Mary was just too heavy for me to bear. And so I didn't even know Little Mary, my own lost child.

When the walking half of me left the bathroom that bad day in 1947, Mom and the ladies in the lunchroom were still laughing and jabbering. I still looked the same. My pigtails, my Cupid's dimple, and my little plaid uniform all remained in place, but underneath I had changed. Mom put her hand on my shoulder and I shuddered. She kept talking and I kept my shameful secret.

For the rest of Mom's life, I was never able to tell her about what happened, what our priest had done to me. She would have cried.

That night at home, things had changed. I didn't crawl up on Dad's lap. Ordinarily, I would have been eager to tell him, Mom, and Nickie about the magical movie machine with the wheels that went round and round. But the magical machine was in the same room where everything unspeakable happened, and I understood nothing of it except that some form of sin or evil or badness had taken place there. I lacked any trace of ability to absorb the experience and just couldn't bring it up.

How fast a moment can change everything. At twelve-o'clock noon on that regular day, my concerns were Mrs. Horn, the mushy peas, Mom, and the lunchroom ladies.

By twelve-thirty it was a terrible day and everything had changed. *I better not tell anyone, God,* I prayed. *Just you. Please bless me, God. Please bless me.*

And still, even in this hour, there was that one miraculous thing; Little Mary had already learned that she was supposed to believe that God knew her every secret and loved her through them and in spite of them. By the second grade, I believed what the nuns had taught me about being friends with God. I talked to God that day as I looked into the mirror because it already came naturally at this early point in life. This was the beginning of an unending conversation. It had begun with the teachings of my faith, but it was sheer necessity that drove me now.

* * *

I needed to hold on to God and at the same time to go away—split, detach, dissociate. I had to stay the same on the outside and hide the inside. I had to keep secrets and be very careful about trusting anyone.

At age seven, these skills—detachment from myself and attachment to God—were my saving grace. They kept me from fading away forever—especially the skill of splitting. It was a natural response that helped when I needed to go invisible, the next time Father Rucker raped me.

3

BROKEN DREAMS

*The dream is the small hidden door in the
deepest and most intimate sanctum of the soul,
which opens to that primeval cosmic night that
was soul long before there was conscious ego
and will be soul far beyond what a conscious
ego could ever reach.*

—Carl Jung, *The Meaning of Psychology for Modern Man*

AS A CHILD, I often had falling dreams. I would see myself falling off a cliff and, just before I landed, my body would stiffen and jerk me awake. I was so scared every time this happened that my heart pounded and I grabbed my blankets and struggled to "fall" back asleep. I went to bed every night with the fear of having one of those dreams. They stopped when I was in my early thirties, but only to change into a new nightmare of a man who was always going to get me.

The man would chase me and I would run and run. Often these dreams ended with me screaming myself awake, a bloody murder kind of scream. They were so vivid and so real, like the falling dreams of my childhood, that I would awaken shaky and afraid, with a pounding heart.

As I began to understand how dreams and especially nightmares might be the result of significant childhood trauma, like sexual abuse, I wondered how my own nightmares could have been a key to unlocking priest abuse at an early age—had someone only asked me about my dreams as a child.

* * *

After remembering that first incident of rape by Father Rucker in the school auditorium, I dreamed I saw myself in his bedroom. The dream was a complete flashback. I saw everything in the room—his chair, his desk, his bed, the window. I was on his lap in a large, padded, leather rocking chair.

Back and forth he went, in and out, like the first time he raped me. In the flashback dream scene, I was in it and out of it. I felt bound by his strong hold, yet looking into the scene, I saw Father Rucker stretch his head to the right, lift it up a bit so that his neck muscles tightened and his eyes appeared vacant as he looked into space. Later, other written accounts by little girls, now adult women, victims of Father Rucker, describe the same tilt of the head and his staring into the distance while he raped and betrayed them. Victims of sexual abuse can often describe the scene of their abuse with accuracy, yet find it very difficult to recall the feelings that accompany the trauma. At least that has been my experience. When the unexpected flashed before me that night, terror, shock, and a sense of acute alertness struck me like a bolt of lightening. Little Mary was shaking and murmuring. I felt her presence and mentally wrapped comfort blankets around her. Grown-up Mary felt repulsed, disgusted, angry.

How could you do this to us? We called you Father.

Maybe that was the moment when some feelings began to return. Maybe Father Rucker was the thief in the night who stole sweet dreams from me and other children. That was the night I really thought what a terrible, terrible thing had happened to Little Mary.

I wondered. Was Father Rucker alive? Was he dead? Where was he?

I use the word *rape* instead of softer words like *molest* or *abuse*, because rape is what it was. In the 2012 issue of the FBI newsletter, FBI Director Robert S. Mueller, III, approved revisions to the Uniform Crime Reporting Program's 80-year-old definition of rape. It reads in part:

> "... rape is 'Penetration, no matter how slight, of the vagina or anus with any body part or object, or oral penetration by a sex organ of another person, without the consent of the victim."

This flashback dream jarred me awake. The images of the place I had been were sharp and clear in that moment. Peaceful sleep stolen by Father Rucker, the thief in the night—a robber, he haunted all his victims. I wondered how Father Rucker slept...or if he did. Where was he? Alive or dead?

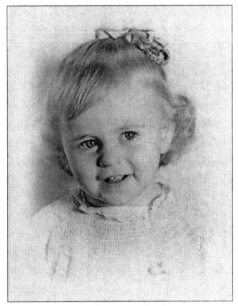

Mary Catherine Dispenza

4

THE OTHER CHILDHOOD

Memories of childhood were the dreams that
stayed with you after you woke.

— Julian Barnes, *England, England*

I WAS BORN ON EDDY STREET in Chicago, welcomed by my mother, Catherine, my father, Nick, and my toddler brother, Nickie. Our family moved far away while I was still very young. And we kept the old black Pontiac that Dad drove from Chicago to California in 1942 for a very long time. Maybe Dad loved that car because it brought him safely to new opportunities and a freedom he had not experienced in Chicago.

Mom did what wives did back then, which was to follow her husband. We kids piled in the backseat among the boxes and bags of our worldly possessions, heading west to the land of promise. Nickie was three years old and I was one and a half. We knew nothing of the California Dream, but we were headed for it.

My earliest memory of losing Mom was when I was about three years old. It was a time of air raids and Victory gardens. Air raids scared me. As each siren sounded, Mom ran around the house, turning lights off and pulling the shades down—those old-fashioned shades that were creamy white and had a string with a little circle attached at the bottom for pulling up and down.

One night I was sitting on the toilet and Mom was helping me, when a siren sounded. Mom jumped up and left me alone, clinging to the sides of the toilet seat while she hustled around shutting lights off and pulling shades down. The bathroom was pitch black. I was afraid. That is my earliest memory of fear.

When I was around seven or eight years old, Aunt Annabelle would take me downtown with her to Clifton's restaurant where the food circled around on a conveyor belt. Fascinated, I watched as item after item passed by like magic, round and round, in and out the window. *How fascinating*, I thought, *they're like a train.* At the time I drew no connection between my fascination with revolving machinery and the whirring, revolving wheels of Father Rucker's film projector.

Even with my favorite aunt, I was a silent kid. Dad and I were alike in this way. He didn't talk much either, but he expressed himself through his beautiful piano playing and song writing.

After lunch with Aunt Annabelle, it was on to the May Company to the fine china section. My aunty gave me a lesson in how to identify fine china—especially cups. She would raise a cup to the light and have me notice how thin it was—so thin that the light came shining through. Next, I listened to the sound as she gently tapped her rose-gold wedding band on the outside of the cup. *Tap, tap, tap.* Then with a sigh, a deep breath in and then the words out, reverent and low, she whispered "*Havilland*" or "*bone china.*"

From there we went on to the yardage store, where I could touch all the fine materials. We rarely bought anything, but I took in the sights, sounds, smells, and feel of everything I could.

Sunday mornings, I strolled down Telegraph Boulevard with Uncle John, going down one street then another, until finally we stood at the foot of a magnificent cathedral. Awed, I always wanted to bow as if I were meeting a king. Inside, as I took in my surroundings, I became smaller and the church became bigger—as if I'd entered a fairy-tale world filled with kings and servants and a banquet table of everlasting food—the Bread of Life. Everyone seemed welcome at this banquet. The statues with their glass eyes, the incense, and the words of Jesus enveloped me. I was at peace in the church—at home. As the golden angels cradled the centerpiece behind the altar, I felt angels hold and cradle me. Nestled against my uncle's side, I drifted on the comforting drone of the Latin liturgy.

On the way home from St. Joseph's Cathedral, Uncle John held my hand. This hand I trusted. We would stop at Patty's Pancake House. I'd crawl up onto a stool with chrome legs and a red plastic top; I'd listen to what my Uncle John ordered and say, "I'll take the same. A large stack of pancakes!" He would pull one curly braid, and tease me. Uncle John looked into my soul and loved me, found me worthy of love whether I felt it or not, but still he did not see the torment nor the source of it.

Mom and Dad didn't go to church. I'm not sure if Mom ever went to any church. And Dad loved Mom more than the Catholic Church, which taught that he could not really be married if he married someone outside the church. He chose Mom and stopped going to church. Dad didn't stop valuing the church and what it offered; he and Mom enrolled Nickie and me in Catholic school and Dad drove us to Sunday Mass each week—a Catholic school expectation. He never went into church. He waited for us. Dad went to work at McDonnell Douglas Aircraft each day. Mom stayed home. As Dad began to make some money, he decided to move us to the other side of town—East Los Angeles—where houses were cheaper. Dad and Mom bought their first small home on Duncan Avenue. Soon the city decided that the Santa Ana Freeway should go through our home, so we moved around the corner again to another small place. Eventually we ended up on a dead-end street, Wilkins Avenue in East Los Angeles. During this turbulent time in my family's life, I entered St. Alphonsus School, and my childhood took a turn.

5

KIDS IN THE HOOD

As a child I felt myself to be alone, and I am still,
because I know things and must hint at things which
others apparently know nothing of, and for the most
part do not want to know.

—C.G. Jung, *Memories, Dreams, Reflections*

THE KIDS ON my block were mostly latchkey kids who played in the street after school, or in the empty lot and graveyard beyond the dead-end of the street. I was the only girl and the youngest kid, who tagged along with the four boys who ruled Wilkins Avenue—Nickie, Peter, Jose, and Zorro.

Nickie was my brother, Peter my playmate. Jose was a high-school kid who wanted to get me to go into the cemetery and take my jeans down so he could see "what a girl looked like," and Zorro was a troubled boy who, even at an early age, seemed only to focus on sex.

When we were young, Zorro begged me to stand with him and watch the pigeons in his cage hump each other and listen to their hissing sounds. One day, years later, two policemen, a mom, a dad, and a teenage girl walked up to Zorro's door. I was sure I knew why. Zorro had raped the girl. He was sixteen years old. *Zorro* is Spanish for fox. I decided right then and there to stay away from Zorro, the Fox.

East Los Angeles was a dark place to grow up, at least in my neighborhood—my dead-end street. On the corner was Vince's

Top Shop. Henry, the upholsterer, lived in the apartment above the shop with his wife and their eight-year-old daughter, Lillian. I heard my mom talking to Patty, our neighbor, over coffee one morning.

"Henry took Danny and Lillian into the Top Shop, pulled down the big metal door, and had them take off their clothes." Little Danny was Patty's five-year-old son. Later, I watched as the police came and took Henry away. Henry was gone for several months and the metal door of the Top Shop remained shut.

I kept my jeans up around Jose. I avoided Zorro's pigeon fetish. I stayed away from Henry and the metal doors. By this time I had my own metal doors to contend with, the sweaty palm of Father Rucker and the shy pride of being walked around the schoolyard.

I never figured out how to stay away from Father Rucker.

There were things missing from my days. Blank spots remained. Some afternoons, half an hour went missing as the unspeakable and unremembered went on and on. I feared the days Father Rucker found me and took my hand—usually at lunch.

He took my hand the way he always did. "How are you, Mary?"

"I'm fine, Father." I wasn't fine. I was afraid. *Dear God, please don't let him hurt me. Please.* Was I alone as he slipped his hand into mine or was I with my playmates?

Father liked the school auditorium, where he sat me on his lap. It had a secret hiding place with doors and mystery behind them. Now, that became a familiar place. First, Father Rucker pushed the swinging doors open and looked at me with that gentle, Superman smile of his. Then, holding my hand, he walked me up the ramp to what seemed like half a floor, because when we got to the top of the ramp the overhead room was not very tall. It was cool and dark, like an upstairs basement. Spooky. Scary.

There were old desks everywhere, piled on top of each other. I could see an old blackboard on wheels by the light of small, dirty windows.

Father Rucker lifted me onto his lap. His fingers began to wander...

I am split in two again.
Old blackboard . . . Dirty windows . . .
Dear God, stop, make it stop.

Finally he led me to the back of the auditorium and left me there in a daze while he casually walked away. This happened again and again. Was I eight or nine years old by then? It always took me awhile to reorient myself.

Where is the play yard? Is it lunchtime? Where am I supposed to be?

Eventually, afternoon classes started and I got back to my desk, but trying to learn was futile. My brain was still whirring, grinding away on the lost experiences, trying to find some way to cope with what they left behind . . .

* * *

Little Danny was five years old on that hot summer day, small and malleable. Since I was a few years older, Danny was someone I could have power over, and I knew that he'd already been behind closed doors with Lillian. And so on that hot summer day, I coaxed him to lie down with me. The dry grass was scratchy and coarse. I wanted to touch him. I didn't know why.

"Danny, let's get under my blanket and take a rest."

"Okay." We got under the blanket and, because we were kids, we didn't last more than a minute in the heat and scratchy grass. Nothing happened. I didn't know how to question myself about what I was doing, or think about possible consequences. It was a sudden, overwhelming urge that seemed to pick me up and then set me back down like an ocean surge. Then the urge was forgotten for the time being, and I seamlessly shifted out of the role of secret seductress and back into Little Mary. I did it automatically. The transition was so smooth that I never felt it.

I did a lot of housecleaning, especially in the summertime. Usually our house was a mess. I didn't like that. I needed order around me, so I would clean and clean and clean. No one seemed to mind the mess like I did. I felt better when I cleaned. I took something dirty and made it clean. I helped Mom, who couldn't seem to get it done. By now, Mom was tired.

Sometimes when I was cleaning the front room, I would turn on our old Philco radio/Victrola, pick out some of Dad's LP records, and set about three of them on the spindle. I would click the lever and one record would slide down to the turntable. Then I'd pull over the handle ever so gently and place it on top of the record. The music began to play one favorite after another like, "Cruising Down the River on a Sunday Afternoon" and "I Could Have Danced All Night." I grabbed the broom and held it as if it were Fred Astaire and I were Ginger Rogers. Dancing converted the boredom of summer into joy.

The empty lot at the end of our block had a huge dome-like bush that was hollowed out inside. It was shaped like a teepee. Often I would crawl inside this hidden space, break off a dried piece of vine—we called it grapevine, maybe it was—take a pack of matches I snuck from my mom's purse, and light up my grapevine, my "Lucky Strike," like Mom smoked. I wanted to be like her and close to her. It was my secret place where I talked to myself and prayed to God. It was a miracle that the bush and I didn't go up in flames. But it was a place where I was safe from Father Rucker, and that was good.

"Hi, God—I like it in here. It is my secret hiding place. Thank you, God."

There was something about being in that bush all alone that felt comforting. Perhaps it was the fact that I could control my surroundings there, talk to God, and with each puff of grapevine, hold on to Mom for a while longer.

6

UNBREAKABLE CONNECTION

*But the last one: the baby who trails her scent
like a flag of surrender through your life when
there will be no more coming after—oh, that's
love by a different name.*

—Barbara Kingsolver, *The Poisonwood Bible*

I WAS MOM'S LAST baby. I heard Mom say that she could not have any more children. I never knew why and I never asked.

Mom drove the school bus and worked part-time in the rectory counting the Sunday collection money and doing secretarial work. She probably never imagined that the same priest she worked for in order to send her children to Catholic school was raping her little girl. We both wanted to believe that Catholic school and the inside of the church were safe places for me.

Overnight and on weekends, the old yellow school bus sat outside in our driveway. It gave me a sense of importance. No one in the neighborhood had a mom who drove a school bus. I was proud and she was sober, responsible, and productive.

Mom was still the wispy, lanky, beautiful Mom who dyed her hair from brown to black along with the other bus drivers, Mrs. Brown and Mrs. Miller.

Each morning, my brother, Nickie, and I, dressed in our Catholic school uniforms of navy blue and white, would jump into the bus and pick any seats we wanted. No other kids had this opportunity, this chance to walk up and down, row after row, testing out and choosing the perfect seat.

Mom drove down Olympic Boulevard with purpose. She had work to do. I knew each stop by memory. I could have driven the route myself, had I been older.

I watched intently as each child got on the bus. Something in my heart stirred deeply as, every morning, a gray-haired grandma helped a little girl onto the bus. The little girl had a big round face and red hair with a bow that pulled it back from her lightly freckled face. I noticed that her face was so, so round and her eyes were different, a little slanted, and her large head sat right down on her shoulders. Never did she sit with anyone and never did anyone sit with her—including me. I was in the third grade, she was in the fourth.

At lunchtime one sultry day, I skipped around the chain-linked fence that encircled the swimming pool in Atlantic Park, across from the school. Dirt was kicking up behind my brown leather high-top shoes. The sun was beating down on me. I was about to round the corner when suddenly I saw a group of first and second graders standing in a huddle. I couldn't see what everyone was watching. I squiggled and wiggled myself through the crowd and there before my wide eyes was the little red-haired girl.

She was on the dusty ground, her back against the chain-link fence that encircled the swimming pool. Her navy blue skirt was pushed up and the tip of Matthew Barron's crutch had pulled down her panties. He had had polio and should have known better. He was poking and jabbing at her "down there." Everyone was laughing. Watching her torment, I connected with her. I knew I loved her. She needed help. I ran to tell Sister. But Sister Beatrice didn't listen. She was busy ringing her little bell with the black handle. She said, "Go play." I was so sad. I couldn't help my little friend.

Later I learned that the little red-haired girl had Down syndrome. In those days we just called her retarded. After that, I formed an affinity with the little girl with the red hair. I loved her from a soft spot in my heart. I never showed her my love and she never knew that I tried to stick up for her on her very bad day. I wish somehow she had known that I loved her then and now. I wish that I had sat next to her on the bus.

It's strange that I didn't talk to Mom about the little red-haired girl. This little girl captivated my heart and yet I didn't talk about her to anyone. Maybe this story was too close to my own at the time and my shame too great about it all. Maybe I believed that if I shared this story about the red-haired girl, Mom would figure out that someone had hurt me "down there," too.

7

THE CLOTHESLINE

*I am afraid. I am not solid, but hollow. I feel
behind my eyes a numb, paralyzed cavern, a
pit of hell, a mimicking nothingness.*

—Sylvia Plath, *The Unabridged Journals of Sylvia Plath*

I WAS NINE YEARS OLD on a sunny Saturday, a washing and hanging out the clothes sort of day. The summer sun was shining down on me in my white T-shirt, the one that was a little small. My jeans were a little small also, showing my white socks and those tall, brown oxford shoes that Nickie and I had to wear until the fourth grade, because Grandpa was a shoemaker and he said high-top shoes were good for our feet.

So far, nothing was unusual about this day. I was sitting on the black rubber tire seat of the swing set Dad had made out of some steel pipes and cement, down at the end of the dusty driveway near an apricot tree at the side of our house. The apricot tree and swing were very near the rectangular slab of cement Dad had poured to give Mom a platform to walk on while she was hanging clothes.

The whole clothes-washing routine on Saturday was amazing and predictable. Monday through Fridays, Mom worked and I went to school. Then on Saturdays, we two females were home together. First Mom collected the clothes from everywhere in our small house. Then she carried the basket to the storage garage and the sorting began. White clothes. Dark clothes. Towels. Sheets. All sorted. Then, pile after pile, clothes were washed, rinsed, and finally wrung out, before being hung out to dry. Mesmerized, I watched as soppy, wet items were inserted carefully between two rubber rollers while Mom turned a crank handle that scrunched the clothing until every drop of water was squeezed out and each item looked like a flattened cartoon character run over by a tractor.

At last it was hanging-the-clothes time.

Mom's apron pockets held a zillion clothespins. I followed her outside. This was our special time. Her hands would dive into her apron pockets and pull out a clothespin or two and begin to link one piece of clothing to the next along the line. I was swinging. Mom was speaking, telling me a story about what happened at work.

Back and forth, back and forth, the swing made its hypnotic motion as I kicked the dry, tan earth beneath me. Then I twisted and turned the chains holding me. Tighter and tighter I wound myself, then swirling and twirling, I unwound myself, gaining momentum, reveling in the feel of air on my face, head flung back, daring the dizziness to take me. I became a yo-yo, surrendering to the spin. I could Rock the Baby, Walk the Dog and do Around the World. I could make the little wooden disk do amazing tricks and then, when it was too tight, I would unwind the string and let the whole mechanism find its point of stillness. Like a yo-yo, I spun within the chains of the swing, winding and unwinding, watching the ritual of Mom and laundry.

"Mary ..." Mom called my name. My head was going round and round. I tried to listen while she talked on, but I couldn't hear her. The words were jumbled, running into each other, spilling and spinning into nothingness, as was I. I could not make any meaning from the string of sounds that came out of her mouth and got lost in my spinning. I was scared. Something strange was happening and I didn't know what it was.

I can't hear, Mom. I can't hear, Mom.

What did you say, Mom? What did you say?

I was losing my connection to her—there were no clothespins to stay connected.

She repeated the words again for me. They faded. I faded. I couldn't ask her again to repeat the words. I was gone. My voice was gone. I tried to call out to her. It was like in a dream, when my mouth made a scream with no sound. To keep myself from falling into nothingness, I repeated over and over again, inside myself, *You heard Mom, you heard Mom, you heard Mom.* But I hadn't heard Mom.

I was afraid. I didn't know what was happening to me. I wasn't sure where I was or that I was still on the swing. This time was different from the day in the little bathroom. I had the feeling that I just might take both of my half-selves and leave for somewhere—nowhere. Part of me seemed to be with my Mom who was hanging clothes. The other part of me—I didn't know where it was.

I wanted Mom to stop hanging clothes. I wanted her to come over to me, take my small hands into in her warm, soft hands, and ask me, "Honey, what's the matter? I'm here. Don't go away. Tell me what you're feeling. I love you." I wanted her to know I was broken. I wanted her to put me back together.

She didn't come for me because I couldn't call out and tell her I had spun too far, that I'd become a yo-yo, gone "Round the World." My hands clung to the chains of the swing; my mind was breaking apart and terrifying me. My hands: my mind. My body: my voice. Myself: my mother. Bit by bit we were losing each other, spinning away. I could not understand any of it.

* * *

I lost connection with Mom again one night when I awakened and felt she was gone. I wasn't sure if I was dreaming or not. I tiptoed to Mom and Dad's room. I peeked in. Their bed was empty. Maybe she and Dad were around the corner at the tavern on Olympic Boulevard, the one that I passed by often on my way to the store. I went to find them. It was eleven o'clock at night.

I pulled the heavy tavern door open a crack and looked into that dark place. I heard voices talking to each other and smelled smoke. This was not a place for me. A man came to the open door and asked, "Are you lost, little girl?"

"I'm looking for my mom and dad."

He shouted, "Hey, there's a little kid out here looking for her mom and dad."

Mom came to the door and took my hand. Everything was good again. I had Mom's hand. She had mine. We didn't say much on the short walk around the block to our house. Mom didn't seem upset that I went to look for her.

"I was afraid," I said.

She smiled and we kept walking home.

Of course Little Mary had no idea why she felt such a strong need for mothering. I began to gravitate more and more toward the nuns who taught me. Year by year, these loving women at school were present with their love and attention. They filled Mom's shoes, to a point. They genuinely cared for me and represented a mother-like image and a godliness that helped me feel safe. The nuns taught me a belief system that I needed and were the reflection of God for me. Not one of them ever pulled me into some secret place and used my body for secret gratification, and yet along with their loving attitudes, they nevertheless imparted messages that diminished me further and added to my shamed self.

My seventh-grade teacher taught us that an "illegitimate" child was one born to parents who were married outside of the Catholic Church. My heart shuddered. Mom and Dad were not married in the Catholic Church.

The thought "I am illegitimate" became bigger and bigger until it braided into a new belief: "I had no right to be born." The words haunted me.

I prayed every day at daily Mass after receiving the bread of Christ, "Please God, help my mom and dad get married in the Catholic Church."

Then one day I got up enough courage to ask my mom to marry my dad in the church.

"Is it really important to you?" Mom asked.

"Yes."

"Your dad and I can't be married in the church, because I was married once before I married your father." In those days, the Catholic Church forbade divorce and second marriages.

I was crushed, and believed myself forever illegitimate. I was saddened, too, that my mom had to bare her secret to me: When she was young, she ran away one night, married, then got very sick and returned home to her mom and immediately got divorced. All this happened in a matter of days.

Just before marrying Dad, she tried for several days to see the parish priest, knowing how important it would be to Dad's family for him to marry in the Catholic Church. The answer she received was "Come back tomorrow. Maybe Father will see you then." But the priest was never available and so she gave up trying to get her first marriage annulled.

Dad got angry at being "jerked around" by the church and they decided they would just get married by a justice of the peace. That's what they did to achieve their own acceptance.

I felt indignant on Mom's behalf. It wasn't fair that she had to carry the weight of not being able to do something that mattered so much to me, just because of an adolescent mistake. She wanted to make it better for me, I know. I loved her all the more for that.

Still, I didn't want Mother Anne Marie to know that I was an illegitimate child. It became another secret and another conflicting message.

I would recite to myself, "If I am made in God's image, then I am legitimate." But then another voice would say, "Yes, you are made in God's image and likeness; nevertheless, you are an illegitimate child." I didn't know what was true. Still, no matter what the church said about my mom, she had my heart. I felt certain the church was wrong whether I could explain it or not.

The emotional pain Mom carried was written on her face. It was her physical pain that I did not understand. There were days when Mom would scream in pain. Something on her side just below her stomach—I think it was her right side—caused a violent cramp. She would grab my hand and place it on the aching spot and ask me to massage the spot vigorously. I could never quite do it well enough to ease the pain. Then she would say, "Go get Patty." Patty was our neighbor and Mom's friend. I would run as fast as my legs would carry me. Mom was so pretty, so frail. I had to take care of her.

"Patty, Mom needs you. She has that pain."

Patty and I scurried back to our house. I watched as Patty could do what I could not—take my mom's pain away.

By the time I was eleven, Mom was finding other ways to take the pain away. Every night I was her liquor store companion. Three quarts of Eastside beer in brown bottles was her drink of choice. It later progressed to cheap wine, and then good old Jim Beam, Ole J.B.

One day when I was angry about her drinking, I cut a picture of her in half. It was my way to get rid of Ole Jim Beam. In the photograph, Mom was sitting at the kitchen table. The right-hand side of the picture showed her hand holding a glass. I took the scissors and cut off the hand holding her drink, trying to get rid of Ole Jim Beam. Of course that didn't work and Ole J.B. was always at her side, especially in the later years of her short life.

I split Mom in two, just as I had split myself in two. We tried to live within our pain, but we couldn't make it better for one another.

We even sought comfort in one another's pain, though I didn't realize that and I'm sure she didn't, either. Damaged people often find ways to seek each other out, trying to ease loneliness and fear. Mom and I were no different. Maybe that is why I could never let her go.

Nickie and Mary with mom, Catherine

Mary and Nickie with dad, Nick

Nickie and Mary with the old Pontiac

8

ERASED

Touch has a memory.

— John Keats, *Lines to Fanny*

GEORGE NEVILLE RUCKER, a native of Iowa, was born in 1920. Times were hard for Iowans before the Great Depression began in October 1929. In the 1930s, many families in the United States, especially farm families, experienced serious economic challenge. As World War II began, many men went off to war; Rucker went off to the seminary.

He entered St. John's Seminary in Camarillo, California in 1941, at age twenty-one. He spent his summer breaks from 1941 through 1945 at his family home. He was ordained and assigned to St. Alphonsus School in East Los Angeles, as associate pastor, in 1946.

It was one year after his ordination to the priesthood, when he was twenty-seven years old, that Father Rucker held me and forced his fingers into my vagina. Was I the first of his victims? Had Father Rucker any prior history of abusing children? Did church officials know about his propensity to molest young parishioners before assigning him to parochial schools? My own question remains: Why did the Catholic Church allow Father Rucker to walk in and out of children's lives, raping and abusing them, for over forty years? Why was he not defrocked instead of just being passed on from parish to parish?

The Father Rucker I see in my mind is tall, well built, with a head of dark hair, rimless glasses, and is handsome in a Superman/

Clark Kent sort of way. Maybe he thought he was a super man in having power over me. I thought he liked me.

Father Rucker abused me until I was in the fourth grade. Then, in the fifth grade, Mom left her bus driving and church work to make more money at another job, and Father Rucker left me. Was I too old for him to mess with? Did puberty scare him away? He was, like the neighborhood kid, Zorro, a crafty, sly fox. Whatever the cause, Father Rucker loosened his grip on Little Mary, who was becoming an adolescent, to take the small hand of another child into his.

I later learned that Father Rucker saw a therapist in his early years of raping children and that the therapist told him "the child would forget." I suspect this was said to make Father Rucker feel better. On record with the Archdiocese of Los Angeles is proof that Father Rucker raped or sexually molested thirty-three little girls since 1947. This is only the tip of his iceberg.

Father Rucker remained in the parish for the next two years, but not in my mind. I had erased him, dissociated as I was from much of day-to-day reality. Is it any wonder that a child would want to forget childhood abuse, keep it secret and buried? Years may pass before the secret surfaces. That's how it was for me. In most states, the laws and statutes of limitations around the crime of sexual abuse protect rapists instead of their victims. The disregard of the reliable fact that child sexual abuse can be forgotten for years is unconscionable. Recently, the Catholic Church has been leading a quiet battle in state legislatures around the country over abuse cases and the statutes of limitations. The church authorities don't want to face the fact that child sex abuse often remains buried for many years. If they did, there would be so many more suits to settle and that translates into paying out even more money to deserving victims.

Father Rucker was transferred to another parish when I was in the sixth grade. I never missed him. Good-bye, Father.

But then he showed up again.

9

I ANOINT YOU

I sign thee with the sign of the cross.

—From the rite of Confirmation

IN THE CATHOLIC CHURCH, there are seven sacraments. Six sacraments are available to everyone: Baptism, Penance—or Reconciliation as it is now called—Holy Eucharist, Confirmation, Matrimony, and Last Anointing. The seventh sacrament is reserved for men like Father Rucker, who want to be priests. It is the sacrament of Holy Orders.

Confirmation is the sacrament that makes children about to be adolescents "strong and perfect soldiers of Jesus Christ." Generally, the Archbishop administers the sacrament. In 1953, Archbishop James Francis McIntyre of Los Angeles, soon to be Cardinal, came to St. Alphonsus School to administer the sacrament of Confirmation to my seventh-grade class. Unbeknownst to me, Father Rucker returned from Mary Star of the Sea, a nearby parish in San Pedro, to assist the Archbishop.

When the day arrived, the seventh-grade girls and boys of the parish marched into a church crowded with relatives and friends. We filed into the fourth row from the front—boys on the left and girls on the right. All the boys were in dark slacks and white shirts and ties; I was dressed like all the other girls in virginal white. I hated the stiff veil bobby-pinned to my hair, but I wanted to look like an angel. Mom and Dad and Nickie and Aunty Annabelle and Uncle John were all waiting for me to be confirmed. The church's magnificence shone for our special day.

The altar was bright with gold candelabras holding long white candles that drew me into the flames. Flowers flanked each side, and the smell of incense and blossoms floated through the air. The Archbishop delivered a sermon. I do not remember his words, probably a speech about growing up in faith and armoring ourselves with God's protection. We had been prepared by our teachers to answer any of the questions the Archbishop chose to ask us as a sign of our readiness for the sacrament of Confirmation.

Once the sermon and questioning were over, the anointing ceremony would begin. It had a militaristic tone. Ellen, my chosen Confirmation name, was printed on a small card and handed to the Archbishop. I chose Ellen for an aunt I barely knew. She was Uncle John's sister and I loved Uncle John. Since I could not take the name John, I chose a name very close to his. The Archbishop would dip his thumb into a little bowl of sacred oil called Holy Chrism, a mixture of olive oil and balm, usually blessed by the Bishop on Holy Thursday. With his oily right-hand thumb he would draw a cross on my forehead as he said the words over me, "Mary Catherine Ellen, I sign thee with the sign of the cross and I confirm thee with the chrism of salvation. In the name of the Father and of the Son and of the Holy Ghost."

The anointing of my forehead with Holy Chrism was a reminder that I, as a Christian, was confirmed and must now openly profess and practice my faith. I could never be ashamed of it and would never deny it.

Shame. I was about to feel it wash over me.

After pronouncing my Confirmation name, the Archbishop would give me a slap. As described in the catechism, it was a little tap on the cheek, to remind me that I must suffer for the sake of Christ.

After the anointing and the slap, an assistant priest holding a small piece of cotton would wipe off the Holy Chrism. One assistant priest stood on the left of the Archbishop for the boys

Confirmation Day, 1953

and the other assistant stood on the right side for the girls.

It was time to kneel to prepare to walk up the altar steps to the Archbishop. At this moment, the assistant priests, who had been kneeling off to the sides, took their places. There before me, on the girls' side, stood Father Rucker. Seeing him, my insides rebelled. I was flooded with shame. Voices swirled inside my head, confused, anxious voices.

That man hurt me!

But—how?

I panicked.

I need to get out of here. How can I get out of here?

You have to stay here, another inner voice said. *This is your confirmation with God. You cannot run away.*

Jumbled thoughts and feelings swirled and whirled in me. I wanted out of that place. I pleaded with God:

Get me out, please. I don't know how to get out. Help me God.

But I was locked in again. I had to go to Father Rucker. My heart was pounding. Racing.

Then, everything in the church slowed as I walked up the altar steps and approached the Archbishop. I knelt before him. He pronounced my Confirmation name, anointed my forehead with Holy Chrism, and gave me the gentle slap I expected. I knew the slap was coming, still it was a surprise—it woke me from the trance of ritual, from the intoxication of candles and incense, from the jumble of my panic. My eyes were open to the moment.

This was the man! Father Rucker!

God. God. His hands. I know these hands.

Closer and closer, he reached to touch me and my past bubbled to the surface. I closed my eyes as his thumb rubbed, in slow motion, the sign of the cross from my forehead. He wiped the Holy Chrism from my forehead. I let him touch me in front of everyone. In front of God. Time stood still. Still. The scent of the oil of chrism wafted over me. I knew him and then, with the wiping away of chrism, I no longer knew.

Confirmation was the first and only wake-up moment I allowed to surface for more than thirty years. For an instant, when I was thirteen, I knew Father Rucker had raped me. I had words now, for that part of my body and for the acts he had perpetrated on me. Street words, tough East L.A. kid words. Shame washed over me. Did it wash over him? Was he ashamed? Did he even care?

Almost instantly, again, I split from that knowing. Splitting was the only way I had to stay in the glow of the candles, the music, the incense, the prayer, the love of the nuns. The only way I knew to be the child of God and the warrior for the church. But spirituality, sexuality, and shame were forever fused within me in that sacramental moment.

I walked out of church that day "a strong and perfect soldier of Jesus Christ." I loved being good and the affirmation that came with that. It was easier than clinging to the memory of rape. In order to survive, that day in 1953, I turned away from all memories of Father Rucker and left them at the altar. At the age of thirteen, my subconscious knew how to survive. It split, and I forgot.

Mom, Dad, Aunt Annabelle, Uncle John, and my brother, Nickie, celebrated with me. We probably had a picnic. I probably had ice cream. The sun was probably shining. But I came away with no memory of what we did or how I felt. Again, Father George Neville Rucker had stolen any emotion of joy that could have been mine. For the next thirty-six years, I remained split. My child self simply chose to forget.

It may be possible that what the psychologist told Father Rucker—"The child will forget"—was true. But the forgetting is a terrible rending in which the child tears herself in half, deserts the half of herself that holds the memory, and continues on with only the fragmented self that does not remember.

A few months later, I gave the dress I had worn for Confirmation—the assumed white purity of preadolescence—to Martha, a classmate who was poor. I thought maybe she needed a pretty dress. Maybe this was my way to turn a very bad day into a good day. Looking back now from the perspective of my wholeness, I can only hope she wasn't raped before she got to wear it.

Father George Neville Rucker

10

SCHOOL DAZE

I thought how unpleasant it is to be locked out;
and I thought how it is worse, perhaps, to be
locked in.

—Virginia Woolf, A Room of One's Own

I TOLD THE WOMEN in the circle about my call to the priest. They
were silent. Every one of them breathed a sigh of relief when I
added, "I hung up." No one wanted to confront her abuser—at
least not until we were on very steady ground and had the support
that we needed.

I sat on the edge of my folding chair, anxiety oozing out of
me. Maybe I didn't have to go it alone. For the first time, I was
on my way to unlocking a great big secret that made intimacy
impossible and kept me living life as if split in two. I wasn't
whole. But now I was sitting with other women who all knew
one commonality: we were survivors, or trying to be.

In that circle I began to talk about a subject that I had never
addressed before. Perhaps it was the same for some of the other
women that day. I was so anxious. My eyes seemed open more
than usual. There I spoke the first words of my experience and
heard myself say the phrase—"childhood priest abuse." I had yet
to descend to the depth of emotions I harbored within. Some of
the experiences I could face and recall. The emotions I could not.

Sadness snuck in at age seven along with the invasion of the
priest's fingers. Fingers pulled out, but sadness stayed in, as did
isolation, abandonment, and shame. It may always be there. My

life work has been to come up from that well of sadness and stay out of it for longer and longer periods.

Many women shared their sadness in the circle. I didn't. I listened, took it all in, and remained detached from my own pain. Detachment from myself and compassionate focus on others had always worked for me. I could think of others and leave myself behind. Detachment coupled with the desire to serve made me a perfect candidate for the Christian way of life. From the outside, I was a shining light of joy and effectiveness.

Splitting myself provided me with an amazing ability to live effectively in service while hiding wounds and shame. It served me well in the circle also. That is, until a women asked, "Mary, aren't you angry? Why do you keep working for the church?" I froze on the spot. These were two questions no one had ever asked me before. I couldn't answer. I wouldn't answer. I retreated inside to my soul place.

I believe we each have a soul—the core of our being, the center of love, grace, and all that is good. My soul was the place that I fled to each time my body was invaded by the priest. My soul was strong and safe. Father Rucker did not steal my soul. In fact, it was my soul—my God place—that saved me from total isolation after his attack. My soul kept me alive and yearning for wholeness and health. Choosing to keep my soul as my sacred place saved me, but I was not free from sorrow.

When I was in the first grade, before I was split in two, I remember learning about my soul. Mother Beatrice, my first grade teacher taught me messages from the Baltimore Catechism that I remember today:

"I am a creature composed of body and soul and made in God's image and likeness."

"God made me to know, love, and serve Him and to show forth His goodness and be happy with Him forever in heaven."

"God knows all things, even our most secret thoughts, words, and deeds."

I learned to pray in the first grade in Catholic school. It is fair to say that as a child, God became my lifelong companion and friend. God loved me as I was.

Each school day began with morning prayers, facing Jesus, who hung on the cross over the blackboard. I thought the crucifix was a reminder to be very good and obey Mother Beatrice lest I too be placed upon a cross. The pledge of allegiance came next; with my hand over my heart, I faced the small flag on the thin, round black stick and began, "I pledge allegiance to the flag . . ."

Then in unison we all said, "Good morning, Mother Beatrice."

And she said, "Sit down children." I sat down, moving to the left so as to leave a little room for the guardian angel that Mother Beatrice told me was always at my side. I named my angel Raphael.

First grade was a skipping and jumping time—a time of learning and laughter. It was a time for playing with my little friends and helping my friend Charlene with her reading. I sat behind her, and when it was her time to read I'd whisper to her the words that she didn't know how to pronounce.

"Go Spot, go. Go, go, go."

First grade held clear days of learning. What I took in, I could give back.

It was a happy year at school and a weird year at home in my neighborhood, with strange kids like Zorro and no friends like me to play with.

In the second grade, though, learning became hazy. My school days turned to a daze of disconnection that continued for a very long time. My biggest challenge was taking the information presented to me by my teacher and transforming it into knowledge that made sense. I took the information in, but I couldn't give it back in any orderly fashion when called upon to speak in class, or later to write compositions. Subjects like history and geography, along with lengthy written summaries, tripped me up. The information seemed to lock itself away.

Teachers never seemed to notice, or simply overlooked my learning blocks, because I was a "good" girl, a spirited girl who excelled in school leadership and sports. I wasn't failing. Though I knew I was falling short of performing well, I did well enough for the teachers not to notice.

I sat distracted and "away" through each lesson presented. Learning happened, I just couldn't get it out in a comprehensible way. It would be graduate school when these skills finally fell into place. Until then, I experienced education with the same kind of disconnect I had in other dimensions of my life. Everything was fragmented except when I could use my hands to create and my body to engage. Art, spirituality, sports, dance, leadership, and causes to rally around were the threads that held me together.

Art brought me peace. Sports brought me connection. Dancing and music brought me joy. To relieve my sadness I sought out places and ways to be creative. Through creative acts, I was able to rise up out of sadness. I believe that art is a spiritual act that transcends the realm of earthly things. And sports gave my body a healthy, safe way of expressing myself. Belief in the Blessed Mother, the Mother of God, gave me a mother to turn to in time of need. One thing I knew for certain—the Mother of the Lord Jesus, Mary, was my mother and cared very much for me. While I watched my own mother sinking into alcoholism, this belief comforted and sustained me. Mary as the mother of God and of the Church was a strong piece of my spirituality that helped me feel less alone. Today, that great woman in church history remains a model, inspiration, and companion on my journey.

Dancing let my heart soar as my body moved to the rhythmic beat of rock and roll. These were the days of "Shake, Rattle and Roll" sung by Bill Haley and the Comets and "Walking My Baby Back Home" by Johnnie Ray. I loved those songs. I passed many summer days away dancing the bop. In spite of the inner death I had endured, I needed to find ways to express life.

11

SEX IN THE HOOD

*For every sin there is forgiveness and especially
for the sins of youth.*

—Marcel Proust, *Within a Budding Grove*

SUBCONSCIOUSLY, I KNEW about predatory men, though I didn't know I knew. Some Saturdays I would walk to the show, as we called the movies then. It was a long walk, three miles or so. If I saw a man walking down the same side of the street I was on, I would cross to the other side to avoid him. A simple walk through a neighborhood one day had resulted in a man grabbing my undeveloped breast as he passed. I pushed his hand away, then couldn't get to the other side of the street fast enough.

While the kids in the neighborhood were tuning in to sexual experimentation, I was having my own struggles. Jesse, a boy in the neighborhood, would gather us together in a dark, empty garage with an unlocked sliding door. Since we were latchkey kids, no one ever really knew what we did each day between school and family supper times.

Behind those garage doors, kissing and touching went on. I went once, but I was shy around sexual stuff. My emotions were jangled when I came too close to it and yet I wanted to be like the other kids.

I knew I was different from the other kids. For one thing, as a bed wetter until I was in the fourth grade, I had learned not to go to sleepovers. I learned that lesson while spending the night with a friend and awakening to a wet bed. It embarrassed me to the core. My friend had a cat, and I tried to blame the cat for the wet spot. I knew no one believed me.

I started touching myself in the fourth grade, after Father Rucker left me. In the seventh grade, I learned a new word for touching myself. Masturbation. I couldn't stand the sound of the word. It was a strange word. Master what? A man. A mister. A master. As much as I disliked the word, I couldn't stop doing it. By night, in order to fall asleep, I would quietly slip the blankets between my legs and move back and forth, back and forth. Silently. Silently. Then a tightening, a gathering of all the energy I had in my body, and a feeling would spring through me as little lights flashed through my brain. Finally in a heap of exhaustion, I slept. All in secret, all without sound, such a pleasant, shameful experience took place. Father Rucker gave me this habit and he gave me the shame that accompanied it every morning after. But I didn't know that then, either.

During the lonely summer months, I looked for other ways to stimulate myself, like finding things to rub against my body. I did not understand this compulsion, or why I knew how to do what I was doing. I couldn't stop myself. Then of course, the shame followed. *I have sinned. I have sinned. I have sinned.*

The sacrament of Confession was the only way to rid myself of guilt for this devastating sin of pleasuring myself. Masturbation. It is quite possible that I confessed this sin to the very priest who raped me. He had his own confessional with his name above it. Father Rucker. Denial kept me from making any connection between this man-priest—the man who raped me—and my own sexualized compulsions for release of desires I should not yet have known I had. Sexuality, spirituality, and shame, twisting and turning, became entwined like the braids on my head.

When I was about twelve I wanted to look like the other girls I had seen in the theater, with their bandanas pulled back with bobby pins, a white blouse, tight jeans, and white baby doll shoes. I would carry my red silk bandana in my jeans pocket along with some bobby pins and make my long walk up Eastern Avenue, a scary street that butted up against the cemetery. Then, I would turn right down Whittier Boulevard. It was the main street in town with shops and theaters lining both sides. I learned to be intentional about safe streets to walk. I stopped taking short cuts and back streets.

The familiarity of the stores on Whittier Boulevard—Kress's, Grayson's, Woolworth's, the stationery and art supply shop, and the pet shop—kept me grounded. I knew exactly on which corner the Beech Nut gum machine with the shiny metal rectangle could be found. You put a penny in, pressed one of those levers down, and a little flat piece of gum would come out. I didn't go for the gum, though. I went for the shiny metal front that let me look at myself. I would take out my red scarf and bobby pins and go to work. I pinned my scarf back on top of my head, pulled each side forward and pinned again, and then pulled it back and tied it, letting the corners hang down. Now I thought I looked like the other girls who sat in the show waiting for a boy to sit next to them and make out.

Then, there in the theater, that feeling of things slowing down and fading out would come over me. I was there and I was not there.

My friend Brenda looked more the part I was trying to play. Maybe that is why she got the cool Cholo boy with the khaki pants and white T-shirt to sit by her and I got the less cool and milder-mannered boy who simply held my hand. Brenda's guy was gyrating up and down with his head as his tongue thrust into Brenda's month. He must have been seventeen. Brenda was fourteen. He asked her to meet him in the alley behind the Bank of America on Atlantic Boulevard. She said his tongue made her sick to her stomach. I never knew if they met in the alley. A part of me wanted to know, and another part of me did not.

I wanted that secret movie-time life, but those hours in the darkened theater gave me a headache and made me ill. So I'd come home, grab the bottle of Anacin, pop the lid off, and take two tablets. It seemed to work for Mom and Dad; it would work for me. Soon my headache was gone.

I have tried to remember what movie I was watching at the time Father Rucker first abused me. I cannot. I can see the old movie machine with the two big wheels groaning as they spun continuously, the imagery transporting me away from the knowledge of what was happening to me.

As a pre-teen, I walked around within myself—separating my secret self from my outside self. Sometimes I would wear my "incognito disguise" when I came home from school. Somewhere I found an old hairnet. I would put my long hair into the hair net and bobby pin it in four places, then don my fluorescent pink baseball cap. My jeans were rolled up at the bottom and a long watch chain was clipped to my belt loop and hung down into my pocket. My fluorescent orange shirt over a white T-shirt finished the outfit. Maybe costume is more appropriate. In this guise I felt safe for a while. Butch. Tough. A tomboy no one would threaten. Sometimes dressing up like this seemed strange. Maybe, after all, it wasn't so strange or crazy. Maybe it was smart. Maybe I was smart doing what I needed to do to hold myself together. I wanted to disguise myself—be someone else for a while—not the girl with a secret. I had to stay away from the secret and the shame that bound me.

One day when I was in high school I disguised my voice like a boy and started my confession to the priest, "Bless me Father for I have sinned. I touched a girl."

I was uneasy and very shy about my body. Never did I intend what had happened that night.

Margaret and I had slept like "spoons," so close and tight that a mighty explosion erupted in me. It had to do with my body and was so pleasurable that it must be a sin, I decided.

We were both kind of skinny girls, so we just cuddled in together. I'd been touching myself for several years…this night, I wanted to touch her and for her to touch me.

The priest asked, "Did you lose the seed?"

Not knowing what this seed thing meant, I said, "Yes." I knew something had exploded within me. I knew the night had been long and sleepless. I knew we hadn't actually done anything and weren't even sure what we wanted to do. Just something.

The priest spoke one sentence, "Don't ever do that again."

I answered in one sentence, "Yes, Father."

That's it, nothing more? No lecture? No words of wisdom?

In my own wisdom, I figured out that even with the sin of the seed, it was more acceptable to be a boy touching a girl than a girl touching a girl. Telling the priest about girls touching each other would have been the greater sin. Girls cannot love girls. Margaret asked me to spend the night again. My response was, "Only if I can sleep on the floor." I did sleep on the floor. Margaret hung her arm over the side of the bed so I could hold her hand. That way I did not commit a sin.

Shame. Shame. *Shame on you.* This echoed constantly in my head. Shame always accompanied anything to do with my body, or with sex and sexuality. Putting on my gym suit in front of other girls in high school caused me such anxiety and embarrassment that I dreaded going to PE, even though I loved athletics.

From the sixth grade on, Mom was working at Lifschultz Fast Freight Company in West Los Angeles and Dad still worked at McDonnell Douglas in Long Beach. Dad was getting home later and later and Mom was drinking more and more. I now dreaded my nightly trip with her to the liquor store for her three quarts of beer.

Nickie hung out with the neighborhood gang, but he had friends who went to the Mormon Church. There, we discovered families that provided activities such as dances and parties for their sons and daughters. The price for participating in these activities was attending prayer time. I never did, but my brother went, so I tagged along after him to the events. No one ever questioned me.

Sex in the Mormon Church seemed alive. At least the birthday party I went to one evening, for Nickie's friend, Nellie, was filled with kissing and touching games. I was twelve. I'm sure my brother had to take me with him to the party for some reason. He and his friends were older. We played Spin the Bottle, my second experience watching kids kiss kids. The finale of the game time at Nellie's party was Seven Minutes in Heaven. This sounded like a religious game to me. Not so. And all three of the qualities I carried with me through life were there also: spirituality, sexuality, and shame. The Mormon spirituality, teen sex, and of course, at least in my case, shame.

While the parents were in the kitchen, supposedly chaperoning, the twelve of us went into the bedroom and found places to make out. Imagine! Paired up boy and girl, girl and boy—the Mormons drew the line at same-sex coupling. I wanted Nora to be my partner that night. I was comfortable with her. By design, I was given the creepy seventeen-year-old Louis. Now I felt trapped again.

The lights went out and for seven minutes everyone touched, kissed, and touched and kissed some more. Louis was insipid. I hated every moment. He was homely, had zits, was too skinny, and was generally unattractive. The same familiar feeling of being trapped and of wanting out left me spinning in my head. I couldn't stop thinking that Marilyn, the popular one, was always paired with the handsome boys. *I'm stuck with the ugly one.*

This was not the end of Louis. Oh, no. He knew a good catch when he stumbled onto one. I got a phone call soon afterward. It was creepy Louis.

"Can you go to the drive-in theater with me and Sam? Sam is taking his girlfriend."

I didn't know how to say no. I always had a difficult time saying no. I called Mom at work and asked if I could go to the drive-in with Louis. She said yes and she would meet him when he came to pick me up.

Sacred Heart of Mary High School, 1958

This was a very bad decision for Mom to make. Louis was seventeen and I was twelve. I needed some help from her to say no. After telling Louis yes, I worried.

Maybe Louis will do more than just kiss me. He may hurt me and take advantage of me. What if I can't say no, tell him to stop and that I don't like it? What do I do then?

Shy and afraid, I got in the car with creepy Louis and David. David had a reputation for being a good guy. We drove to David's girlfriend Teresa's house to pick her up and meet her mother. Teresa's mother was smarter than mine and more protective. She smelled a rat and said no. I envied her ability. Just saying no is not so easy after someone has taken your voice away. I had to relearn the skill and had a long way to go.

Now I was in the front seat with Louis and David was alone in the backseat. Another movie. Another whir, whir, whir of the projector. I started spinning again. I don't remember the movie itself. Louis kissed me and kissed me. I felt sick. He unzipped my jacket, unbuttoned my white blouse, slipped a hand in, and touched my small breasts. I became an observer. Watching from the outside, I waited and wondered where his hands would travel next.

Mary and Nickie and the Lavender Chevrolet

At intermission I went into the bathroom. Not a small bathroom, like the small bathroom where I went to wash myself after Father Rucker raped me, but a large bathroom with several stalls. As I sat on the toilet, a sense of strength and dignity came over me. I straightened my blouse, zipped up my jacket, and decided that when I returned to the car, he could not, would not, harm me.

"Dear God, help me to say no. I can't stand his tongue going into my mouth and his hands touching my breasts."

When I returned to the car, David sat in the front seat and Louis pulled me into the back. I sensed that the hunt was on, but I was not going to be easy prey. Creepy Louis kissed me. I sat distant, saying no in my own way. He took my hand, placed it on top of his jeans over his penis, wanting me to unzip his pants. I wouldn't. I didn't. When the movie was over of course, Louis took David home first then drove on to my place. It was now about midnight. I got out of the car, but creepy Louis was there in a flash to push me against the car and press his body against mine. He did not get what he wanted. That was the end of creepy Louis. Thank God.

Mom left the door unlocked for me, but not her heart or attention. I wanted and needed her, but didn't want to wake her up after she drank herself to sleep. So I crawled into bed, alone and shaky. I talked to God, who was always there, and I talked to myself.

Mom never knew about that scary date on that very bad night. She never knew how I stood up to creepy Louis in my own way. I was too fearful to speak of sex and shame to her. And thus my silence was as regrettable as the rest of it. I had become a co-conspirator with Father Rucker against myself by helping to keep secrets for my rapist.

Seventh grade brought with it my period. Mom never got to talk about it with me beforehand. Any time she tried, I told her I already knew, which was a shame-filled lie. I had to lie because if we talked about my period we might have had to talk about other things too painful to remember. I just couldn't talk to Mom about anything that had to do with my body or sex. I really knew nothing, but the shame paralyzed me and made getting my period a very traumatic event.

It was after school. Mom was still at work. Spots of blood appeared on my panties. I knew this was the dreaded moment of the beginning of that thing called a "period."

That is about all I knew, period. I had no real idea why or how the whole process connected to my life. I called Mom at work.

"Mom, I'm having my period."

"Is it bad?"

"No."

Mom said, "I'll bring home everything you need."

I really didn't know what "everything you need" meant. Soon Mom arrived with the stuff. She opened a brown paper bag and showed me a small square box with a clear plastic front. I saw a strange elastic band shaped a little bit like a peace sign. I didn't feel peace. I felt shame again. Then the box of Kotex appeared. Mom gave me a fast tutorial and off I went into another small bathroom—alone and ashamed, while Mom shouted through the door.

"Do you need any help?"

"No." I remained locked in and kept Mom locked out. I did need help. That inside voice of me was saying, "Mom, I do need help. Come into the bathroom and help me with this thing." I would have loved to laugh and joke about it all. Instead, these precious moments that ought to have been shared with my mother were stolen, never to be regained.

The shame of Father Rucker's terrible secret seeped into any issue concerning my body. With something as striking as the first appearance of menstrual blood, I was so overcome by the sight of my bloodstained panties that I threw them into the corner of my closet where they lay until Mom found them and scolded me. Of course all that did was cause the shame to mount. The distance between us grew wider. Mom and I were missing each other in those mom-daughter moments that should have been precious, tender opportunities for bonding and learning.

In spite of these ups and downs, I kept my head above water while my soul—what I'd come to think of as my God place—remained steady.

My head continued to struggle with academics. Putting meaning to the work that formal education demanded each day remained a challenge. I was in school, and yet not. I knew I was smart. I remembered being a smart girl. I didn't understand why I was filled with confusion. Why couldn't I remember the facts and figures that seemed so important to academic success?

12

THE GIFT OF SECRECY

Lies and secrets, Tessa, they are like a cancer in the soul. They eat away what is good and leave only destruction behind.

—Cassandra Clare, *Clockwork Prince*

IT WAS FEBRUARY 19, 2011, twenty-two years after that circle of women first met, when I told my story about priest abuse in an interview for KUOW Radio in Seattle. The piece was called "The Gift of Secrecy."

I felt the switches, levers, lights, microphones, headsets, and soundproof walls hold me in place. Though the sound of a projector provokes jarring memories, I have always enjoyed machines and gadgets. It was no wonder to me that I loved this recording room, a place I had never been before.

Reporter Jeannie Yandel with KUOW, NPR's Seattle affiliate, handed me the earphones and said, "Don't be nervous. Just relax and speak as if you are talking to a friend."

I was more than a little nervous; this would be my first time speaking publicly about priest abuse. The interview became a fifteen-minute piece for KUOW, but the conversation itself lasted for two hours.

I answered one question after another until finally she asked one that caused me to stop, almost losing my voice. "Mary, why did you keep the priest's abuse a secret for so long?" she asked.

A small victory at least was that I didn't stop and withdraw, as I had done before when a question got too close to my fears.

And although I wasn't ready to explain my story of being split, the answer I gave her was true.

"I carried so much shame that secrecy seemed the only way to bear it. My church taught me from a very early age that anything to do with sex was bad. So to me as a little girl at the time, it seemed to naturally follow that being touched by a priest was worse than bad; it was too bad to tell. I learned to live with the secret, to actively protect it, actually."

Telling the story to Jeannie and sharing my long-kept secret was freeing. My circle was widening.

Jeannie's final question was striking. "What gifts did you take from the church?" Negative gifts are seldom the topic of discussion, but while her question was direct enough, it was the idea of negative gifts that flashed through me. I had already been speaking about the terror of my childhood and my decades of service to the church, but I realized that I rarely focused on the "negative gifts" of my experience of Catholicism. I had never thought of secrecy as a "gift."

And yet as hard as it was to live with such shame, secrecy allowed me to survive until it was safe to bring the truth out into the light. In later years when the scandal of priest abuse kept on breaking and breaking, I realized I was far from alone. And when this secret was no longer mine to bear in isolation, I began to remember.

Telling a secret that we have kept out of misguided shame is the beginning of freedom. I know the feeling of a closed heart. Secrets caused my chest to collapse inward, and it was such a closed and constricted feeling that it changed nearly everything about me. Sometimes friends would say, "Stand up straight," or "You're not breathing." Comments like these served as reminders that my body was holding secrets and turning inward under the weight of them.

At age seven I learned to keep secrets, not the pleasant little secrets of girlhood games, but the dark and dangerous secrets that you bury in your bone marrow. When I collapsed for the first time in that small bathroom, my little frame slumped and everything turned inward. That closed-in hiding place held me tight for a very long time.

For more than half a lifetime, secrecy and shame were my constant companions. They lodged in me like squatters. Wherever I was, so were they. I never named them. For years I only knew the dark feeling of each. They held me captive and showed up in so many different ways, always keeping intimacy out of reach for me.

Though I am now free from the secrets and shame of priest abuse, I still want to cling and hold on to a secret. I've lived so long with secrets and shame, that it has taken me time to get used to living in the light, exposed, and without my companions. "Hello, darkness, my old friend," sang Simon and Garfunkel. That's how it is sometimes for me.

At times, my own coping mechanisms remind me of the story of the thirty-three Chilean miners who were trapped underground for more than two months. When the miners were finally rescued and saw the light of day, the glare was too bright for them. The men had adapted to unrelenting darkness. They had to wear dark glasses while their eyes gradually readjusted.

Letting go of my secrets was similar to emerging after decades underground to stand blinking in the light. My best attempt at adapting has been to learn to trust the truth and tell it.

During a weekend in prayer and reflection at my friend's getaway house, I came to some conclusions about secrecy. There are four types: group secrecy, institutional secrecy, personal secrecy, and family secrecy. All secrets, no matter what kind, keep us from intimacy and connection.

"Don't tell anybody. It's a secret—just between us." So many times I had heard that in my childhood and felt privileged. "Are you able to keep a secret?" was another question to which I would answer, "Yes." The very word *secret* sets up an imbalance of power.

The one who holds the secret believes he or she holds power over the one who does not. The group secret shared with a few special people connects the chosen few with each other. Teenagers have their group secrets that only the privileged share to gain power over their peers. If anyone breaks the secret, generally they lose their place in the group. Usually, they are sworn to secrecy and share a code of silence.

On a larger scale, the same pattern occurs. The group may be an organization or an institution and, at its worst, the secrets become systemic. The secrecy within the Catholic Church around the sexual abuse of children is an example of institutional secrecy. Priests, charged to protect their flock and bring them into the paddock of the Lord, instead are using their vows of celibacy to hide their sins of the flesh. The sexual secret inside the clergy is so large and the scandal spread so wide that everyone is suspect.

I look back with suspicion on the years I was a parochial school teacher and principal, and wonder if any of the priests who trained altar boys during the school day had malicious intentions. Were some boys raped and then ashamed to speak a word about it? I think so. I wonder if the principal of my Catholic school knew Father Rucker was molesting children. Maybe.

I believe this form of secrecy mandated by the Catholic Church had a convenient, built-in mechanism to protect priests as they told one another of their sinful abuses under the seal of confession.

The entire church system perpetuated secrecy and hid the horrors of sexual abuse. To declare to children "We do not talk about sex" creates a taboo of shame that at best keeps people virginal until the marriage bed and at worst keeps children from talking about abuse, allowing perpetrators to rape and molest with impunity.

Much has been done to expose bishops guilty of protecting and passing on predator priests, and to make public the names of priest sex offenders, which are otherwise hidden and shrouded in secrecy.

I was appalled to learn from attorneys who prosecute abusive priests that priests often know of one another's transgressions, and that pedophiles often share children. Further, in many instances, leaders in the church know the perpetrators and do nothing to protect children, instead protecting priests who come under suspicion and passing them on to new positions or parishes.

Keeping pedophilia and sexual predation a secret allows the institution of the church to continue to appear holy and its priests celibate. There is almost no way to break through the wall of institutional secrecy and learn what is really going on.

Members of institutions trapped in secrecy know that disclosing one member's secret could weaken the position of all, and might cause the group to falter and be held accountable. When the deeply guarded secrets of atrocities and brutal crimes of sexual abuse against children by priests in Ireland were finally exposed, it became clear that hundreds of priests actively covered each other. In situations such as these, an imitation of loyalty develops between and among the perpetrators. Holding on to these secrets gives the group power. The brotherhood, the priesthood, the bishopric, and the Vatican all possess great, accumulated group power and seek to retain it at all costs.

Ireland became the first country to bring the force of national government to bear against the church. The church suffered a near collapse because waves of courageous victims kept coming forward. Good people were appalled and wanted to have nothing more to do with the Catholic Church.

Family secrecy can be similar to institutional secrecy in that the members are a tightly knit group and want to protect each other. Family secrecy can be seen in something as simple as those times that my mom would tell my brother and me, "Don't tell your father." She usually said this when I went into her bedroom early in the morning to kiss her good-bye as I was leaving for school. We knew that it meant Mom was not going to work that day because she had drunk too much the night before and had a very bad headache. Caught in her shame, she thought a secret seemed the likely way out. It was really the way into the dark place of falsehood, creating a little wedge that whittled away at trust and intimacy between us.

It is so common to hear a family member say, "We just never talked about it." It may be twenty years later that a family finally acknowledges the truth that Uncle Bobby had a brother who committed suicide and a sister in a mental institution. Finally someone breaks the cycle of shame and secrecy and the truth begins to put a lot of other things into perspective as well. "Aha, so that's why ..." Communication opens and the family has the opportunity to experience a new freedom in this new process of truth telling.

Personal secrets can range from itty-bitty things to very significant trauma in our lives. An example in my own life of something I want to keep secret is that I get very nervous if I am alone in an elevator with a man. I try to conceal this fact and keep it a secret, but then it holds power over me. I am ashamed that I have this fear. I should be over this; I remind myself that this is not Father Rucker and I am not a child. Once I am able to share these sorts of secrets with a friend, they hold less power over me.

On the other end of the secrecy spectrum are the big secrets, such as abortion and rape, that can keep us imprisoned for a lifetime and get in the way of honest and open communication, holding intimacy farther away. Shame and fear keep us from disclosing the truth of our lives.

Sometimes secrecy is warranted and an inner compass tells us the time is not right, or it is not safe, to tell the truth. Our lives could be on the line if we communicate openly. Sometimes it is just too dangerous to be forthright, like declaring Jewish roots during the invasion of Germany into France, or coming out about sexual orientation while one is young and living in a hostile, anti-gay environment. At times keeping personal secrets may be necessary to survive.

Other personal secrets are so shame-filled that they may never see the light of day. This is an enormous tragedy because of the devastating toll hiding takes on us. We want to get free from our dark secrets, but the fear is too great. We have come to believe that the secret is just too, too bad to reveal.

I believed my secrets of abuse and sexuality fell into that latter category: too horrible to reveal. In my case, I pronounced this verdict upon myself because the Catholic Church had taught me to do so. As a child, I learned that the greatest sin imaginable was to touch and pleasure myself. The name for this was masturbation. While hearing this in class, I had already tucked away the secret that the priest had touched me and pleasured himself.

In some ways it felt like a family secret also, because I'd been taught that I was part of God's family and the priest was God's chosen one, whose purpose was to show the family the way. He was our Father.

To stay in love with the church and hold on to the concurrent goodness I found from the sisters who taught me, I had to completely separate myself from the reality that the head of this household was hurting me. I had to keep the secret—the institutional, group, personal, and family secret that it had become.

13

I HAVE CHOSEN YOU

*The great awareness comes slowly, piece by
piece. The path of spiritual growth is a path of
lifelong learning. The experience of spiritual
power is basically a joyful one.*

—M. Scott Peck, *Evaluating Empowerment*

"THERE ARE THREE STATES IN LIFE," said Sister Agnes, my senior
class teacher. As defined by the Catholic Church there are
three—only three—states worth any thought at all: the religious
state, the married state, and the celibate state. There was nothing
in between. You can guess, of course, which one was the highest
state. Being a child who always wanted to please God and be the
best, I knew the religious state must be the one God had chosen
for me. And given the depth of shame I carried, very possibly I
thought religious life, a pure and healing life.

Since the seventh grade, I had heard God's call, "You have not
chosen me; I have chosen you." These are words I would later
hear over and over again as a reminder to me that God thought
me very special. I was not only chosen to the highest state, I had
nowhere else to go.

Abuse threw me into God's arms and there I remained.
Choosing a life that promised an ongoing conversation with
God was right for me. I felt connected to a loving God even as
I remained disconnected within my split self.

*Dear God, I want to be a nun. I think this is what you want, too.
I want to do good things for others and make the world a better place.*

From the sixth grade on, I went to daily Mass before school each morning. In high school, I would pick up my three girlfriends, Michelle, Sue, and Lolita, each Tuesday evening, in the lavender Chevy I inherited from my brother, Nickie, when he left for the Army. The girls would drop change into the ashtray for the thirty-cents-a-gallon that gas cost back then and we would go to Devotions to Our Lady of Perpetual Help at St. Alphonsus Church. Mary, the Blessed Virgin Mary of the Bible, Mother of Jesus, is known as the Mother of the Catholic Church. She became my mother also. I prayed to Mary often.

Daily, at lunchtime during elementary school, I would skip and run across the crosswalk, enter the parish church, kneel before the beautiful statue of our Blessed Mother Mary. Lost in the warm gaze of her glass eyes, I felt loved and safe. "Thank you for being my mother, help me to be good, to be a good girl. Bless my mom and my dad. Help Nickie to be a good boy."

The Blessed Mother was my mother. I believed she loved me just as if I were her own child.

But as I ran across the street each day, Father Rucker apparently watched me from his bedroom window in the rectory. He looked down on the crosswalk and created a scenario out of my daily ritual.

One day after school, Mom said, "Mary, Father Rucker asked me if you are hurting down here." She pointed to her own private area. My cheeks flamed with embarrassment. I imagined his conversation with my mom:

"Catherine, is Mary all right? I saw her grabbing herself between her legs as she was running across the street. Is anything hurting her there?"

I was so ashamed.

"No, Mom," I said. "I just was pulling at my panties." Then again we relapsed to a place of shame, secrecy, and silence.

I imagine Mom was very confused to have such an intimate question raised by a priest. Did she wonder why he was watching me? Did she think it strange at all? Was she too captivated by his godly persona to ask more questions? Did she suspect that he was hurting me? I will never know. This was one of Father Rucker's grooming tactics, an essential part of a perpetrator's way of setting up his prey. There he was and there was the safety of the church I was running to, side by side.

I couldn't stop running across the street, even though preying eyes may have been upon me. Crossing the street was the only way I could get from the schoolyard to the play yard and, more important, to church for a lunchtime visit to do my own praying. Child prays, priest preys.

I was always running to God. It is no wonder I entered the convent after high school, at age eighteen.

One afternoon around the end of my senior year I told my dad about my decision. It was a Sunday and though he never attended church himself, he often dropped me off for service and picked me up afterward. After church, Dad was waiting for me. I got in the car, took a deep breath at the next stop light, and said:

"Dad, I'm going to be a nun."

Shocked, he started to go through the red light then stopped himself, backed up, and ran into the car behind him. Stunned by the thought of losing me so soon, he became agitated. He may have considered my entering the convent a possibility yet we had never spoken about my future after high school.

He knew I was serious.

"What about college?"

I didn't know what to say. Dad was a quiet, solitary man. He called me his "breath of fresh air" at home but had never affirmed me, so I never really knew the depth of his love or his pride in me. He finally showed it in the anxiety my announcement caused.

Dad told Mom. Mom questioned me. All the questions came spilling out.

"What about marriage? What about children? What about college? Can't you wait?"

I had no words to respond, which was nothing new. Once again, I locked myself in a small bathroom—only this time it was the little bathroom in our house. I cried. I didn't want to come out. I wanted my mother to hold me and say, "It will be okay. We can work this out," but that moment never arrived.

In an all-out effort to keep me from entering the convent, Dad had various Catholic colleges send me information and enrollment packets. My parents' last effort to persuade me not to enter the convent was to fly me to Chicago, alone. It was the summer of 1958, the time of Chevy convertibles and poodle skirts—the bop and swaying back and forth to slow music on 45'. My mom's sister, Aunt Sadie, told Mom that there was a great boy my age, named Seth, living in the flat above her and Uncle Harry. "Why not send Mary here for a few weeks, maybe …" Of course, maybe we would fall in love.

Aunt Sadie was tall and graceful, her hair silver-gray and her skin like milky cream. Uncle Harry was short, shorter than I was. He mostly wore only a white undershirt with suspenders on top, with glasses on his face and a cigar in his mouth.

Seth, the boy upstairs, was handsome as promised. Though just graduated from high school, he already had a new 1958 Chevrolet convertible and a job in a corporate building downtown. The convertible was white and coral with big fin fenders at the rear. The whitewalls wore chrome hubcaps that dazzled in the summer sunlight. Aunt Sadie told me that Uncle Harry gave Seth the talk: "Whatever you do, if you get her pregnant, I will kill you."

Seth was a serious guy, tall and clean-cut. I found him attractive. He had a great smile and gentle ways. His skin wasn't light and wasn't dark; it was a golden tan color. Seth took me everywhere. We drove out to Skokie, a suburb of Chicago, to see the new homes they were building. He already had one picked out to buy. He let me drive his new convertible with the top down, to a picnic his graduating class was having. He talked about settling down and having a family—and he was only nineteen.

Seth and I did nothing more than kiss under the moonlight on the deck of the third-floor flat. I had never been kissed under the moonlight by anyone. Seth invited me up to his family flat to see his home and his bedroom. He showed me where he kept his money, his books, and his study place. A beautiful moon lit the night sky. Seth pulled me to him and then ... I was afraid. I could do nothing but be apprehensive and scared. I remained passive. Seth kissed me softly. His lips were soft. I gave nothing in return.

And another night came, just before my three weeks ended and I was about to return to Los Angeles, when Seth asked me to marry him.

"I want to marry you," he said.

"I can't, Seth. I really like you but I want to be a nun." Seth knew I planned to enter the convent so that was not a surprise to him. He didn't ask why. I'm not sure what I would have said if he had.

On the day I was leaving, Seth gave me a beautifully wrapped present. It was large and heavy. I had no idea what it was. I opened it. It was a beautifully bound Bible. Inside he had written: "To Mary. Love, Seth." I treasured the gift. It reminded me that a very good, and kind, young man desired me. He chose me. I did not choose him.

Mom and Dad timed my trip to Chicago perfectly so that I would have little time to get the trousseau ready for entrance day. There was no help to ease this process. Every possible roadblock was put in my way to make it nearly impossible. Time was running out.

14

ENTERING THE CONVENT

You are not on a journey to God; you are on a journey WITH God.

—Steve Maraboli, *Unapologetically You: Reflections on Life and the Human Experience*

MOM DID HELP eventually. She took me shopping for strange items. I think secretly she enjoyed getting a glimpse into a very different way of life—something very much out of the past. There were Dr. Scholl's shoes, the black, two-inch, lace-up kind; long, black cotton stockings; garter belts; long cotton underwear; T-shirts; bras; a petticoat; a black pleated skirt; a long-sleeved, black seersucker blouse; a short cape; and a white plastic collar and cuffs. Also, for yard work days, a blue gingham apron; for bedtime, a long flannel nightgown and a bed cap. This was quite a change from my shorts, bare feet, sleeveless blouses, and baby doll pj's. Ah yes, and there was the set of engraved sterling silverware and a white napkin. Mom couldn't get over this.

"Why not stainless steel?" she asked. Custom and class within convents demanded otherwise.

Dad's way to cope was to keep things inside. The night before Entrance Day, Dad finally burst out with the words he had been holding back.

"Why do you want to enter the convent? It's a waste of your life. What about going to college or getting married?" Dad looked at me, his eyes were begging for an answer that might give him some understanding.

"It's not a waste, Dad. I want to do this."

It was a sunny summer day in September of 1958. Mom and Dad reluctantly drove me to the novitiate in Santa Barbara, an exclusive and wealthy beach town a hundred miles or so up the coast from my East L.A. childhood home, for Entrance Day. This day marked a significant change in my life. I don't think my parents or I talked all the way from Los Angeles to the Santa Barbara novitiate. *Dear God, I don't want to hurt Mom and Dad. I wish we could talk. I want to say so much out loud but I can't. Can you please help me?* The silence was familiar to me. I don't remember any real conversation that had ever taken place between Mom, Dad, and me. Dad was the silent one, at least at home. Mom was the one always longing for his touch, his smile, and conversation. I was the one longing for outwardly loving parents.

A winding pathway lined with dazzling blue agapanthus led up to what seemed like a mansion to me. It was a beautiful estate given to the Sisters of the Sacred Heart of Mary and named Marymount, Santa Barbara.

Flowers were everywhere on the Marymount estate grounds. Birds of paradise, favorite flowers of mine, with their orange and periwinkle blue and pointy beaks, stood tall and proud everywhere. They offered balance and contrast to the agapanthus. Together they spoke to me of elegance and beauty far beyond the streets where I grew up.

The grounds were magnificent. The lower grounds encircled a beautifully designed swimming pool and bathing house. The main house or mansion was on the upper ground level. Attached to the house was a small, intimate chapel where I would pray daily for the next two years, but even that was majestic. The whole scene spoke of wealth and affluence and felt very incongruent with vows of poverty.

Clearly, we all felt out of place, Mom, Dad, and me. We had bid my brother Nickie farewell two months earlier as he boarded a train to join the Army. Now Mom and Dad had to say goodbye to me too.

I wanted to go back home, while at the same time I longed to do God's will. Entering the convent was the right thing, the safe thing to do, the good choice for me. God was calling. Yet I felt out of place in such wealthy surroundings. That old uncomfortable feeling of shame came over me. I was not good enough for afternoon tea and pastries, little sandwiches, a sterling silver tea set. We never had tea in our home at any hour, let alone in the afternoon.

Still, I heard God calling, reminding me that he was my salvation—a stronghold that gave me comfort—my true love, my companion, my confidant, my anchor. If this convent was where God lived, then I wanted to live there also.

I kissed Mom and Dad good-bye and did not see them again for six months. That was the rule for postulants to help us get over our homesickness. Mom and Dad got in their car and drove away. That was it, nothing more.

The Mistress of Novices gathered us up like baby chicks—all thirteen of us. We walked up the hill from the main house to a smaller house, beautiful with its Spanish tile roof and luscious landscaping. Sprays of bougainvillea, stunning pink and purple, draped themselves everywhere. The house was stucco and painted a flat white against which the bougainvillea blazed. This was a welcoming sight framed by the warm, blue, summer sky. I had never seen houses like that in East Los Angeles. Already I was in a different world. Paradise.

Our destination was the garage, of all places. I was suspicious. Then my eyes fell on trunk upon trunk. Mine was a cheap blue one with brass-plated tin hinges. I spotted it immediately. We were each assigned a helper, a novice who had been a year in the novitiate and had taken her first vows of Poverty, Chastity, and Obedience. My helper was Madame Eleanor.

"This is the moment, Mary," said Madame Eleanor. "You have to take your clothes off and put on your new set of clothes." We were getting rid of the modern dress that represented worldliness

Mary as postulant, Santa Barbara, California, 1958

and donning monastic clothing that represented the past and a break from the world. Madame Eleanor wasted no time. Off came my dress, underwear, everything as we both tried to cover me up while it all was coming off. I felt stripped. Naked. A mixture of feelings swept over me. First laughter at the thought of putting on such strange-looking clothes, then a gripping fear and shame at the thought of taking everything off and feeling naked settled in. All that was familiar was taken away. In that moment, vulnerability returned; a shame deeper than the ocean washed over me for reasons I could not have explained to myself or anyone else. Then, in an instant, I left that piece of me behind

Mary, a novice, Madame Marie Nicholas, in Santa Barbara, California, 1959, with Dad, brother Nickie, and Mom

once again; this place of shame was impossible for me. As quickly as I felt the shame, I split from it.

Mechanically, I submitted to the process. I put on a new bra, the knee-length cotton underpants, garter belt, long black cotton stockings, petticoat, short-sleeved cotton T-shirt, long-sleeved black seersucker blouse with slip-on-and-off white plastic cuffs.

Then the black Dr. Scholl's shoes—something a spinster would wear. (Certainly, Dr. Scholl never had to wear them or he never would have designed them.) Next came the black cape with a zipper front and white plastic Peter-Pan collar and a black gabardine skirt. Last, a funny-looking black hat shaped like a cigar box, or maybe a Philip Morris hat, was set upon my head. A small trail of decorative black lace was sewn around the brim of the hat and, attached to the back, was a veil that could be thrown over the front to cover my face and humble me in the majestic presence of the Eucharist and the Blessed Sacrament when I went to daily Mass and monthly Benediction. I hated that hat every day I wore it. Was this an effort to cover the past and escape old tragedies?

The only parts of my body that would be exposed during my several years in the convent were my face and hands. Even my face became more difficult to see, as the final habit I wore hugged my face on both sides like the blinkers on a horse. I looked like a little penguin. The sense of safety in the monastic outfit was lost on me, though; the religious custom of covering and concealing my body spoke to me of shame and added to the shame I already carried.

The end of that first day, Entrance Day, the beginning of another world, came quickly and abruptly with night prayers and the start of what I later learned to observe as the particular silence. This serious quiet is also known as the grand silence.

After night prayers, I was ushered from the chapel to the dorm, two large rooms with about eight small beds in each, white walls and white spreads. A novice introduced as Madame Victoria led me to my bed. Now I panicked. I didn't know what to do. Should I take my clothes off? What should I put on? Where should I put my clothes? No one spoke. The novices chanted a series of Latin prayers. I was nervous ... I was afraid. I eyed my long, white flannel nightgown and bed cap already strewn across the bed. My robe, stark and black, looked dead upon the white of it all. Black, white, black, white. After the glorious color outside, the absence of color inside weighed heavily upon me.

There was nothing to do but get undressed. I was shy and strangely ashamed. Madame Victoria, one of the novices, grabbed my black robe purchased from Nally's Religious Goods store, and threw it over my head. There was no talking permitted in the particular silence. I quickly got the message. Modesty demanded that I dress and undress under my robe. A part of me was relieved to hide under the black robe and another part of me felt oppressed by the darkness and weight of it. Everything that night, and for the next fifteen years of my life, was shrouded in silence.

The silence was easy for me. I had lived an interior life for so long already. I was used to talking to myself and praying to God. So in that way at least, the convent life fit me.

During those two years in the novitiate, my understanding of spirituality and my connection to God grew. Meanwhile, the strictures of the convent further arrested my sexuality and the teachings deepened my shame.

The everyday activities of high school life that had saved me from going deep inside myself were absent from novitiate days—no dancing, sports, student council, or service activities to hold me together. Instead my days were filled with prayer, silence, manual work, and short periods of recreation. Touching myself sexually had tapered off in high school, but it was there from time to time. After entering the novitiate, such touching was relegated to my past. For a time I willed it away. Split again. So much of what sustained me was replaced by a strange and new style of living and loving God.

I didn't miss Mom and Dad. I really wasn't aware of feelings at that level of connection. I didn't know love that binds and sustains. I didn't know love that cries when you say good-bye or jumps for joy when you say hello.

15

RITUAL AND ROUTINE

Be not forgetful of prayer. Every time you pray,
if your prayer is sincere, there will be feeling
and new meaning in it, which will give you
fresh courage, and you will understand that
prayer is an education.

—Fyodor Dostoyevsky, *The Brothers Karamazov*

SO MUCH RITUAL filled each day. In a way it was comforting, and in another way, unimaginative and predictable. Even breakfast was a ritual, with filing into the refectory, retreating to our assigned places, saying the blessing, opening our white linen napkins and placing them carefully across our laps then, lining up our sterling silver in perfect order, like little soldiers, and passing food zigzag across the table.

We ate all meals in silence unless some brave soul went forward to Mère Maîtresse who sat at the head of the main table to ask her or maybe beg for permission to talk during the meal. The first time and only time I had enough courage to ask permission for the group, I scooted my chair out from the long dinner table, took a deep breath, and walked forward until I reached the head of the table, then knelt down beside Mère Maîtresse.

"Mère Maîtresse, may we please have permission to talk?" I said, so low that she had to turn her head toward me to see and hear me.

"What did you say, Mary?" She hated it when we muttered.

I cleared my throat and said as clearly as possible, "Mère Maîtresse, may we please have permission to talk. It is the feast of the Immaculate Conception."

For this exception to be granted, there needed to be a "good" reason, like the feast of St. Nicholas or of the Virgin Mary. A long wait followed, probably thirty seconds. It seemed a lifetime while Mère Maîtresse weighed the merit of this request. The two tables lined with novices and postulants waited like children until she spoke the magic words, "Yes, you can go out and play,"—only our words were *"Benedicamos Domino."* These words uttered by the novice mistress gave us the right to speak during the meal. And when we responded *"Deo Gracias,"* or "Thanks be to God," we meant it.

I never got up the courage to ask permission for the postulants and novices to talk during meals again. Claiming my voice and confidence would not come easily.

I prayed the time-honored prayers with a confident voice unlike the weak voice I displayed when speaking alone. I welcomed common prayer times when in unison we prayed the rosary. Rosary time provided the backdrop for darning the holes in our black stockings. "Hail Mary full of grace the Lord is with thee …" As my fingers glided from bead to bead and I circled from beginning to end, my mind would unwind like a top, freeing itself from the confines of a taut string wrapping round and round me.

Afternoons in the novitiate were spent doing manual labor and gardening. I was given a long white porch to keep clean. It was white-painted cement and about sixty feet long. I would get on my hands and knees and scrub and scrub until it was shining. A good part of my convent years were spent on my hands and knees scrubbing chapel floors as the Sacristan.

The white porch was attached to a beautiful gray stucco house next door to the main house of the novitiate. We had our daily classes there and some of our novices and young sisters slept there. It was warmer and friendlier than the two-story estate house with the red tiled floors, white walls, and tall ceilings, where we prayed and said the rosary and where every whisper became an echo. I longed to be chosen to sleep in the only private room for two in the smaller stucco house. In the dormitory, my shyness about my body, made getting dressed and undressed painful, despite the black robe.

Around four o'clock every day, an hour's meditation was scheduled. We would file into the chapel, very quietly find our place and kneel down. Most of us slipped into slumber, especially after three hours of manual labor. An hour can be a very long time in chapel. The chapel was small, ornate in its décor and yet elegant in its simplicity. In a way I looked forward to our chapel time every day. I felt safe and equal to each novice and postulant. The quiet time of reflection was a part of the day that I relished. I have always liked to pray.

Once a week we would join the professed nuns down the hill in the main chapel to chant the Little Office of the Blessed Virgin Mary. Each postulant had a turn chanting short prayers in Latin. When it was my turn to chant a prayer, I was beyond anxious. I was petrified. I don't know what made me so nervous. No one else seemed to be as nervous as I. When the time came for my part, I stepped out into the aisle with the other two novices. Each of us had a short prayer to sing. My voice quavered and shook. My hands shook. My knees shook. Actually, all of me shook. The bareness of the novitiate took my confidence away. There was no escaping from my fears, loneliness, and shame. Having little to go toward and nowhere to hide, I felt exposed.

Still, I could not understand this severe reaction and response to the task of chanting a short prayer. It did bring back a childhood memory of being coaxed to come out from hiding behind the kitchen wall to sing for company one evening as Dad played the piano. I just couldn't do it. The sense of failure I'd felt then, as a child, was once again present in these moments of shame as a postulant.

Otherwise, I was at home in my place in the chapel. Having a place, even if it was in the chapel, became important in convent life. There was nothing that belonged to me. Anything that I had was always described by the French words, "*a l'usage de*," meaning for the use of, and in my case, "*à l'usage de Madame Nicholas.*" I wrote this on the inside page of all the prayer books I used. Madame Nicholas was the name I was given at the time of my first and temporary vows. The vow of poverty was the driving force behind this rule that nothing was owned by any of us. Everything was shared in common.

After the hour of meditation, we filed into the study hall and proceeded to do our homework and preparation for the next day's classes. This was also time for bathing. Once a week we had an assigned bath time of half an hour. I always lived in a certain amount of stress, so I found it difficult to just relax and enjoy that half hour. I felt compelled to undress quickly, get in the bath, wash, and dress quickly, then get back to study hall. Much of this pressure I placed on myself. I just couldn't calm down or take it all in stride as some of the other novices and postulants did.

The time for study was usually a blur. The same habits I had around study up to this point remained—it was unfocused, fragmented, and unproductive time. Mostly, I dreamed away study time as I dreamed away classes in elementary school and high school. My mind wandered out the beautiful bay windows of the living room of the small white house, which had now become the classroom, and into the garden of roses and beyond. Roses. Beautiful yellow roses.

When a handsome male teacher named Dr. Butovechio came to teach us, I sat mesmerized by his presence. He scared me, though he did nothing to evoke this feeling. Looking back I think it was the fact that here was a male teacher in charge of me just as the priest had been in charge. I surveyed his body from head to toe, stopping at his genitals. I wanted to have power over them and yet at the same time the past still had power over me. I made no connection with my abuse. In fact, I was not sure where my feelings came from. I told Mère Maîtresse about these feelings and she listened compassionately. We both were speechless over the fact that looking at Dr. Butovechio, tall, male, and in charge scared me. His body scared me. He loomed over me.

Mère Maîtresse reminded me that Dr. Butovechio was a good man and a kind man who would never, ever hurt any of us. I could not make sense of my fear of him. I did not continue in his class. I was given a study time instead.

The novitiate was such a different world for me that I lost the footing and grounding I had created from the ordinary everyday things I surrounded myself with before entering the convent. The silence and rituals deepened my soul, yet my body remained detached—and there was nothing to bring the two together.

16

LET US PRAY

Prayer makes your heart bigger, until it is
capable of containing the gift of God himself.

—Mother Teresa, *Secret Fire, Joseph Langford*

DAYS CAME AND WENT, marked only by the seasons of the liturgical calendar. Advent and Christmas, Lent and Easter held the most dominant positions in the church calendar. Advent was a time of silence and simple acts of kindness with a focus on the anticipation of the birth of the Lord, Jesus Christ. As a postulant or novice, all of my mail was withheld during this time. Mail too had to wait for the birth of Jesus.

The Lenten season was equally intense. This was a time of denial. It was a time to make sacrifices and do penance. The focus was on the sufferings of our Lord Jesus Christ. We were called as Christians to identify with Jesus during this time and to find ways to make sacrifices and walk the path of suffering as Jesus had. As a little kid, I would "give up candy," as we would say. The emphasis was always on giving up. In religious life, the word became *denial*. I found many ways to deny myself.

Weeks before Lent, we began to make a whip-like object called the Discipline. Rosary time offered the perfect opportunity to braid and weave cords together, one strand over another. Three strands, like the pigtail braids I loved in my childhood. I made six individual braids about eight inches long, knotting each one every inch or so, then wrapping them together with cord to form a handle. The knots would make each whack to our skin more biting. This sounds sadistic, and yet in the early church this form of discipline was done in a spirit of atonement and mortification—a necessary practice on the path to holiness.

After evening prayer every Friday during Lent, we would walk down the long hallway with the red Spanish tiled floor and high, white plastered walls to the semi-dark kitchen. It was empty and barren, painted a soft yellow. There was an eating nook to the left and the moonlight shone through the multi paned glass windows. On Friday nights, this kitchen became the place for the Discipline.

In a scene worthy of Hollywood, the postulants and novices, lifted two layers of long skirts, unhooked one black stocking from their garter belts, dropped the stocking to the ground, then knelt in the pitch dark and began to beat the inside of their thighs. It was a frenzy. As we hit our thighs, we recited the "Miserere," Psalm 50. *Miserere mei, Deus, secundum magnam misericordiam tuam.* "Have mercy on me, O God, according to Thy great mercy."

I wanted to be a good postulant and imitate the early fathers of the church in their mortification and denial. I beat the inside of my thigh as hard as I could, often to the point of waking up the next morning to find a dappling of purple spots. I always wanted to do my best and in this case even my best seemed not hard enough. Discipline and denial appealed to me. I thought that the more they functioned in my spiritual life, the purer, cleaner, and holier I would be.

Years later, after I left the convent and was having dinner with two of my friends from high school who had also been in the novitiate, the topic of the Discipline came up. I mentioned how awful whipping myself was. They responded in unison, "Did you actually do it?" It had never occurred to me not to. Eilene and Donna, on the other hand, had been much more sensible than I and had little need to prove themselves to be perfect nuns. We roared with laughter over how gullible I had been.

I was so impressionable. Every day at Rosary time, we would

take turns reading and listening to *The Spiritual Life* by Adolphe Tanquerey. Over and over again we read stories about mortification and blind obedience. A story about a monk who was told to water a dry stick every day inspired me. His story taught the glory in blind obedience. I wanted to obey as he did. Then there were stories about denial and fasting. The stories made me want to be like those holy men. Rarely were there stories about saintly woman to emulate.

What might I do to further deny and mortify myself? I decided I would pour tons of salt on my food. No one seemed to notice. The design of our habits and our work to keep our eyes modestly cast down at all times kept us unaware of the people and environment around us. This ritual of mine lasted for several months. Then all food at mealtime became tasteless. I decided it was time to reverse my plan, and so I stopped using salt altogether. I was trying to imitate the saints in my own way.

There was a compulsive strand in me to be good and do the right thing. I learned that the more difficult an action was, the more meritorious it had to be. Unless it was hard, it wasn't worth doing.

This bizarre effort to mortify myself at mealtime—to really live a monastic life like the early saints—caused me to lose a significant amount of weight and bring my already irregular menstrual cycle to a complete halt for about eight months. Finally I became very ill. My body was in revolt at a way of life that did not work very well for me. It was also my body falling into a depressed state because there were no outlets for it to stay afloat. I simply sank for a while. The novice mistress sent me to bed.

Monique, another novice, brought me my meals and mothered me during those days of depression and confusion. Monique had a maternal instinct. I needed mothering. I think Monique was in love with me. Her caring instinct seemed tinged with a desire to own and love me romantically. Thank God for Monique. Without her love I felt abandoned.

Mère Maîtresse finally took me to the doctor's office. Much

to my dismay, she went in with me, exchanged a few words with the doctor, and then went about her errands. She left me. I lay in a small dark room having my metabolism measured to help determine why I had dropped so much weight. I felt lost. It seemed like a couple of hours before Mère Maîtresse returned.

The doctor asked me questions like, "If there were a box of chocolates in front of you and nothing stopping you from eating as many pieces as you wanted, how many pieces would you eat?"

The truthful answer I gave the doctor that day was this: "I deny myself so much food in order to be disciplined and a good nun that if there were no such expectations, I would eat the whole box."

The doctor recommended that I get as much food as I could tolerate. Overnight I went from being in denial to being satiated. I was told to remain in the refectory after all the other novices and postulants had finished meals to be given another round of food. I gained weight. Not much. Some.

The doctor questioned me about having menstrual periods. They had stopped completely. I had not had a period for several months. More questions were asked. I felt the same shame as I had when my mom found my bloodstained underwear.

"How long since your last period … is the flow heavy or light?" I felt so uncomfortable. As a result of this conversation, I was given daily shots of progesterone to cause my periods to resume. After ten days of injections, my period returned and I felt even sicker and more embarrassed than before. I never returned to the doctor for another checkup. Evidently Mère Maîtresse didn't think I needed another appointment. I suppose in her eyes and those of the doctor, filling me up with food and getting periods to flow meant success. Meanwhile, I lived with that dark secret locked away, even from myself.

For a brief time after my illness, rumors had it that I, Madame Nicholas, was going to be sent home. I did not want to go home and the topic never was addressed with me, but the rumors made me nervous.

One evening after dinner, Mère Maîtresse granted permission for me to have recreation with the postulants from Mexico preparing to become lay sisters who would do all the manual labor in convents. I was so at home with them. We started a game they taught me called *Acitron*. It's a circle game from Mexico involving passing stones, or in our case, spools, around the circle from person to person as nonsense words are being sung, "*Acitron de un fandango, sango, sango…*"

Between verses of the song, my friends began to ask, "Mary are you going home?" I hadn't thought about going home. This was my calling. *Yes, I have been sick but that doesn't mean I am going home.*

"No, I am not going home. Did someone say I was?"

I never got much of an answer. Maybe my friends realized they might be spreading rumors unbecoming of religious life. *Please, dear God, don't send me home. I don't want to go home. I want to be a nun and stay close to you.*

With the help of injections and second helpings of leftover food, I grew stronger both physically and spiritually. I was not sent home. Finally it was time to make my first vows. I would commit myself to God through vows of Poverty, Chastity, and Obedience and become a Religious of the Sacred Heart of Mary. I would be a teacher, as all other sisters were at that time, whether or not we had the skills or talent.

In the small chapel, high on a hill in Santa Barbara, California, thirteen young women, age twenty, consecrated their entire lives to God forever. Our parents sat behind us and watched. My own parents, trying to make sense out of it all, had little heart in this ceremony. After a few prayers and a sermon of sorts on young brides of Christ, we were swept away to put on a new and final habit. This habit was much more severe, more binding.

Quickly, my head was shaved and a *certette*, or skullcap, was tied around it. A handmade white cotton band about eighteen inches wide was hooked around my upper body to flatten my breasts in an effort to be less worldly and less attractive. A white veil was attached to the outside of the coif with three small pins, one at the top and one on each side. A beautiful silver sacred heart of Mary and a cross went behind my neck, dropped down in front, and was tied in a loop by the center bow of the *pelerine*.

I was ready now to return to the chapel where, as if by magic, this religious garb and the vows I was about to pronounce transformed me into a Religious of the Sacred Heart of Mary. These were my temporary vows. Two years from now I would make my final vows and receive a black veil.

Kneeling before the altar, so bright and glowing from the gold candelabras and a multitude of candles, I said my vows before God, my family, and the community:

"I, Madame Marie Nicholas, promise to live out my vows of Poverty, Chastity, and Obedience." It was a marriage to God and carried the same weight as a Catholic wedding. As I proclaimed my vows, I had a vision. The altar candles began to shimmer and created an immense golden glow, which expanded and enlarged a hundredfold. In this powerful light I became small and humble, finite. This overwhelming awareness that I was surrounded by the brilliance of God's presence stunned me. It was as if, as happened to Mary, "the glory of God shown all around me." I was humbled in the majesty of God's presence and then pronounced Madame Marie Nicholas, soon to become Mother Marie Nicholas.

With the title I became not just a seeker, but a woman committed to God in service and love—nun. Poverty, Chastity, and Obedience would shape me. It was the time in the church, prior to the Second Vatican Council, when the vows were interpreted mainly as a means to a disciplined life.

* * *

**Mary, Mother Nicholas, on her Profession Day,
Santa Barbara, California**

About the seventh year of my fifteen years in community, I became very restless and uneasy. Pieces were not fitting together for me and I felt very fragmented. I was surviving, barely. Though religious life was and is enough for many priests and nuns, for many reasons, it was not enough for me. The vows and living them were not enough for my body and soul to thrive. Such spiritual axioms as "My grace is sufficient for thee" "Store up treasures in heaven," and "All that you have, go sell, give to the poor, and come follow me" rose to the top and took over in me. These scriptural lines sustained me for several years, but eventually, I had to face the truth that I needed more. And yet I did not know what it was that I needed.

Always there was a tape playing inside me: "You don't need that. That's too much. You can't spend money on yourself." Granted, these were not bad messages, but they came from a place of scarcity, deprivation, and unworthiness in me. This form of poverty was not life giving for me. It brought me death and blight of spirit. The vows of Poverty, Chastity, or Obedience, held less and less value in my desire to live a greater, fuller, and more generous life. "I came that you may have life and have it more abundantly." That made sense to me.

Mother Nicholas becomes Sister Mary as first grade teacher and later principal of St. Alphonsus School in East Los Angeles, 1965 to 1972, pictured here with student on All Saints Day

17

SINS OF THE FLESH

My own sin will not hinder the working of
God's goodness.

—Julian of Norwich, *Meditations with Julian of Norwich*

THE EARLY TEACHINGS of the Catholic Church stated that the body was to be denied, controlled, and separate from our spiritual nature. Out-of-body experiences and the denial of bodily pleasure were fostered and developed. Words such as *mortification, denial, fasting*, and *penance* were an integral part of convent life and the early church.

My skill of splitting worked well with this philosophy. Damaged as I was, I was easily able to separate my body and my soul. I kept them at odds with one another, as instructed. The sins of the flesh signified extreme weakness in religious life. Sister Ruth, a sister from another religious order that I took summer classes with, told me about the relentless guilt she carried because while her mother was dying, she was touching herself. She could have been playing tennis or engaging in any other pleasure-filled experience and not felt the excruciating sting and shame of so-called "sins of the flesh." This sin was presented to us as among the gravest. There was no place for self-gratification brought about by touching yourself. It simply was wrong, bad, and a mortal sin.

St. Paul warned about sins of the flesh in Galatians 5:19-21. St. Thomas Aquinas, a prominent doctor of the Roman Catholic Church, taught that masturbation was an "unnatural vice" and a grave sin against nature. *Persona Hermana—Declaration on*

Certain Questions Concerning Sexual Ethics, written by Cardinal Seper in 1975, states that "masturbation constitutes a grave moral disorder," and that "both the Magisterium of the church—in the course of a constant tradition—and the moral sense of the faithful have declared without hesitation that masturbation is an intrinsically and seriously disordered act."

For years in religious life I would fight the unending battle of my spirit at war with my flesh until I would realize they were one and could live in peace with each other. I stopped touching myself completely during the novitiate by self-discipline and self-denial. It worked for a while and freed me from feeling I was unclean and living in grave sin.

The most challenging vow for me was Chastity. The word itself was foreign to me as an eighteen-year-old. It was not a part of my vocabulary. As a postulant, the word began to take on meaning of sorts. In our spiritual reading I learned about chastity belts and thought it unfair for a woman to have to lock away her body until a man freed her. I read about Brides of Christ and sins of the flesh, especially masturbation. Very simply, chastity meant that I could not marry, have a child, or enjoy any sexual pleasure. At age eighteen, neither of these first two options entered my mind. I just wanted to be a nun. I did understand touching myself, and thought that desire for this self-pleasuring act would simply disappear.

As the years went by in religious life, the loss of masturbation as a way to manage stress and tension took a toll on me. It was about the eighth year into my religious life when I finally touched myself again.

The weight of summer-school programs, reading, and homework crushed me. I was studying in my small room. A small bed, sink, built-in closet, and shelves in an eight-by-six rectangular space framed my anxiety.

Exhausted, with books strewn across my bed, I knelt on the floor and returned to a familiar comforting pattern from long ago.

My hand slid into my underpants and found the place I knew as refuge and release. Quickly, it was over, and for a brief moment, I was free from anxiety. A few ragged breaths, and then quickly, so quickly, I was ashamed. I wanted to hide—go away, leave my body behind. I had sinned. I was guilty and guilt ridden. I swore to never touch myself again. Willing away my desires and needs worked for a time. *Please, God, forgive me. I am so sorry.*

The thought of confession haunted me. I had to confess this sin to the priest. I could not. I was too ashamed. I would leave it, forget that it ever happened—detach, dissociate, and disappear. As the years went on, chastity in religious life became a call to exclusivity. God alone was my lover. Intimacy belonged to God. In this most perfect way I was free to serve others completely and without reserve.

In the late 1960s, our order stopped using the terms Madame and Mother and moved to Sister, as it was the more modern way of addressing religious women. I was now Sister Mary. This was the time when Pope John XXIII threw open the windows of the church for fresh air. Things began to change for many religious orders. With these new attitudes came more freedom for sisters. The ways of addressing one another eased, the stricture of time eased; we felt encouraged to combine our ancient way of life with modernized engagement with the world.

Opportunities to experiment with and experience our sexuality became easier. Of course any behavior judged too intimate remained frowned upon. I developed a particular friendship with Sister Phyllis. Her attentions tapped into my sensual self. But the community shunned particular friendships. *The Book of Customs* read "…particular friendships are the bane of communities. They gave rise to jealousy and deceit." Phyllis and I were having one of those.

Sister Phyllis was a young nun, just out of the novitiate. She was sent to our convent and to St. Alphonsus School to do her internship in teaching. I was assigned to her as her master teacher. We spent a great deal of time together. Phyllis observed me every day in the classroom for six weeks, and I worked with her in preparing lessons every evening.

One evening, Phyllis went to bed early because she wasn't feeling well. I stopped in to see how she was doing. I had grown fond of her by now. Her warmth and affection for me were evident, and I liked it. In fact, I wanted to feel it. I was sitting on the bed next to her as we talked that evening. It came time to leave and I placed my hand on her thigh as I said good-night. In that touch we sexually awakened to each other.

The six weeks ended and Sister Phyllis was assigned to St. Alphonsus School. We spent more and more time together and gave much energy seeking times and places where we could touch, fondle, and tenderly caress one another. By day we were both first-grade teachers under the same school principal, Sister Margaret Ann, who may have suspected our love for one another—our "particular friendship."

One evening, Sister Phyllis and I snuck away from a community celebration and went to my small room in the convent attached to the school. We lay on top of the bed and began touching and kissing each other. All of a sudden a familiar sound, the click, click, clicking of Dr. Scholl's nun shoes, came down the narrow hallway, nearer and nearer.

"Phyllis, someone is coming. The door, I need to lock the door."

My heart was pounding. I reached over and turned the button on the doorknob. Locked in and locked out. Closer and closer the footsteps came until finally, the doorknob was jiggled, turned one way and then the other. My heart stopped. I was sure Sister Margaret Ann was the invader. Then the footsteps walked away down the hall.

I took a deep breath and said, "Oh my God, that was scary."

The next morning Sister Phyllis, Sister Margaret Ann, and I all drove to school in the station wagon, pretending none of this had happened. All of us, in our own way, wanted to believe it had not. I was left with guilt and shame.

Not long after this, five of the nuns who taught at the school submitted a request to our superior to do a five-year experiment in community living. It was granted, and Sister Carol, Sister Marina, Sister Phyllis, Sister Colleen, and I, Sister Mary, moved into a neighborhood house. The year was 1970. I experienced freedom in a way I had not when I lived in the convent. We all did.

The nineteen sisters remaining in our community convent found this experiment to be unnecessary and upsetting. The sisters challenged us with questions like, "Why would you want to do this, leave the rest of us here to carry the load of community life? What will happen to the portion of money you are receiving from the parish subsidy? Who will pay rent for your house? You could live here." And perhaps, the most meaningful question, "How will we do without you? We will miss you."

We quickly grew comfortable with our newly found freedom to come and go. We were, for the first time, mostly accountable to ourselves and to each other. The five of us covered each other's backs as each of us stepped out of bounds. It worked, because we were all stepping out of bounds in one way or another. Two sisters were dating priests, another sister wanted to be dating a priest, and I was in love with Phyllis. The experiment failed . . . or had it? In some ways it was a roaring success—if life's journey is about finding out, and living out, the mystery of our lives.

Midway into our experiment, Carol and Phyllis left our small community of five. My heart broke in two when Phyllis left. That is when I learned that a heart really can break. Phyllis had always told me that loving and touching each other was good in God's eyes because we loved each other. Then, she was gone and had a boyfriend.

I was bewildered, lost, and obsessed with the desire to bring her back. I drove to her apartment and sat outside. Crying alone for the love and touch of her, I wasn't sure how to mend my broken heart. Secrecy and shame returned. I could not tell the sisters how my heart was breaking and how in love I had been. I could not talk about it. I had sinned, broken my vows. Made love with a woman.

My teaching suffered and the children lost out. I was usually an excellent teacher. Now I felt the guilt of falling short and cheating the children out of learning. "Children take out your math books. Do pages sixty and sixty-one." I stopped preparing and teaching well. I simply could not focus.

Phyllis finished out the school year at St. Alphonsus, School then moved on. I returned to my coping mechanism of detachment and denial.

The next year I was appointed principal of St. Alphonsus School. Colleen, Marina, and I remained in our rented house, which we now called the Repetto House because that was the name of the street we lived on.

Living in this freer style of community was a continuous challenge to my vow of chastity. Now the challenge was with two male teachers, Mr. Chilkee and Mr. Jinkins. We touched and kissed, sometimes in my school office after hours—sometimes in their cars. The experiment in small group living allowed us more freedom to be absent from the community for moderate amounts of time without giving all the specifics of our whereabouts. I had such a need for physical connection and such an ability to detach and split that the contradiction of my behavior and the vow of chastity and my role as principal never collided within me.

Compartmentalizing my life was what I did best. Having been sexualized by Father Rucker at such a young age, shame and secrecy kept on growing in me. A life of seeking sex and touch, while haunted by shame and guilt—that was Father Rucker's legacy. This was reckless behavior, behavior unbecoming of a religious vowed to chastity. It was wild and adolescent arrested sexual development. I lost my compass and had no healthy way of working through it all.

I knew I was in trouble and I needed a change. Still, I was

not ready to leave my religious life. I needed my sisters and community. I requested a change to Mexico, to the orphanage near the pyramids, where our sisters had volunteered for years. My request was granted and in the summer of 1972 I packed my bag, left my position as principal, said good-bye to friends, and headed to Mexico. I was thirty-two years old.

Dad had always wanted to visit Mexico, so he accompanied me on the flight to my new home, Nuestros Pequeños Hermanos. My dearest friend Sister Anthony and two beautiful local children greeted us at the airport—the *pequeños,* as they were fondly called. Each *pequeño* reached out a tiny bouquet of flowers to us, as a sign of welcoming.

For me, memories of the journey in the old bus from the airport to the orphanage are blighted by the memory of a severe toothache. Second to that was the feeling that Mom was with me, even though she was not. She couldn't make this trip. By now her alcoholism had progressed to the point where she was

Sister Mary, called Madre Maria, with children of Nuestros Pequeños
Hermanos, Acolman, Mexico, 1972

Madre Maria and the pequeños painted the mural,
"De Colores" in 1972. The mural exists today in Acolman, Mexico.

nearly too weak to travel. But the bus was like the one that was always parked in our front yard during my grammar school years. It was comforting to feel a sense of Mom's spirit as the bumpy road led me to my new home.

My toothache throbbed. I was adjusting to the high altitude—a sure sign that I was now in a very different space. There wasn't much talking on the bus. It was a time to take in the air, our new friends, and the environment. The pollution of Mexico City evaporated into the bright blue sky and fresh clean air of Acolman. Huts made of straw and mud replaced concrete buildings. Donkeys passed us carrying loads of branches, jugs, and produce. Acolman was situated at the base of the pyramids of San Juan Teotihuacán, meaning "place of the Gods." I could feel God's presence in the fields and in the visible simplicity of living.

I prayed an inside prayer:

Thanks God, I am grateful for the blue sky, the golden fields of corn, for my dad next to me, for the sisters, and for my life. Bless Mom. Soon a new life will unfold for me. I know there will be children. I am good with children. I place this time in your hands. Show me the way to . . .

"Mary, why did you want to come to Mexico? I thought you liked being a principal."

I turned to Dad and realized I hadn't shared with Mom or Dad the struggle I was having with leaving the convent. It seemed time.

"Dad, I've been wondering for a very long time if religious life is the life for me. I'm just not sure." I wanted to tell him about the double life I was leading and how I had been unfaithful to my vow of chastity. I couldn't. As always, our conversations were short and continued within each of us, silently. Silently.

Our thoughts drifted off. Finally, at the end of the country road appeared a magnificent hacienda surrounded by a high stone wall. The old bus stopped right in front of the wooden door leading into the grounds. A hand-carved sign hung above the door, *Nuestros Pequeños Hermanos*. Many hands pulled the heavy door open and the bus drove through into an immense garden of flowers—pink, magenta, orange, and white—interspersed with leafy green vegetables of all shapes and sizes.

The *pequeños* smiled, helped us out of the bus, and Alfredo, the director, greeted us. Alfredo had a smile that traversed his face from ear to ear, like a half circle pulled slightly to the right. I felt warmth and real joy from him right away. He seemed happy in his work and grateful to have another nun to love the *pequeños*.

The Religious of the Sacred Heart of Mary had a long history serving in Acolman. Sister Antonio, fondly called "*Madre*" *by the children,* became my mentor and model of dedication and compassion. She and I shared a very small dwelling in Acolman, made out of cement, and painted stark white. I grew to love the simplicity and clear mission of loving children into themselves and of giving them an education as a way out of poverty. I taught art to the children and English to the youth, and in the process developed a fondness for the dusty roads, the cornfields, the bright sunshine, the children, and my daily diet of rice, beans, and something from the garden.

Madre Antonio and Madre Maria, amigas en Mexico.

This was my first time living in another country and experiencing another culture. Though there were challenges, I was freed from the everyday responsibilities that went with being an elementary school principal. In the simplicity of living, I found my center again. My God center. The space and pace allowed time for reflection and prayer.

The fogginess began to lift.

By spring I knew I needed to leave my community. It was Holy Week, a very special liturgical time in the Catholic Church. And it was Good Friday when I made the decision. I wrote to Sister Maureen, the provincial superior at the time, requesting that I be dispensed from my vows. She in turn wrote a letter in support of my decision. Both letters were mailed to the Holy Father, the Pope, requesting my dispensation.

From age eighteen until I was thirty-three, the vows of Poverty, Chastity, and Obedience shaped me and held me together. Of course, there was a great price to pay as I gave over my will, body, and soul to my religious community. And yet, the convent may have been just the right place for me at the time. Had I stayed in the world, it is very possible the world might have eaten me up.

The nuns were my mother and sisters. They were my family and friends. They loved me into aspects of myself that I cherish today. I may have broken in two, not simply split, if I had not been held by their love through the years of my brokenness. Today, I still call them my sisters. Many remain among the greatest women I have known. They very possibly saved my life. It's not that I would have taken my life, but the path I chose was an important stepping-stone to eventually finding my true life.

During the last years of my religious life, post-Vatican II theology began to open more freedom for those serving God's people, by moving the emphasis in vows from denial and renunciation to the stewardship of goods and of the earth (Poverty), love of God and others (Chastity), and personal growth and mission (Obedience).

This was the beginning of a healthy change for religious men and women. I would not be a part of it. I left my religious community in the summer of 1973. Fifteen years after I entered the convent in 1958, I was saying good-bye. I was thirty-three years old and moving into a world of which I knew very little.

18

FINDING MY WAY

We have to dare to be ourselves, however
frightening or strange that self may prove to be.

—May Sarton, *Journal of a Solitude*

WHEN FRIENDS ASKED why I left the convent, I simply answered that it really wasn't an outside kind of thing. I wasn't seeking anything outside of myself like marriage, children, family, or sex. I really was seeking peace inside. I had grown so restless and anxious within myself. I felt split and broken in pieces and I thought the way out of this was to leave the convent.

That was my answer then, but now I have come to believe that some of those reasons weren't simply connected to the way of life I was living; they were quite possibly the effects of unaddressed issues and effects of the early childhood rape and betrayal by the priest.

It wasn't an easy decision, to leave the convent. I had talked to God about leaving or staying for the last seven years of my convent life. I wrote and wrote, trying to understand myself. I would sometimes sit in silence for an hour, while my superior waited patiently for me to talk. Unable to put words to my feelings, I felt a deep sense of failure for not being able to give clear reasons for wanting to leave.

Sister Micheal Ann would be so kind and say, "I can wait." Of course, she could only wait so long. After five or so years of trying to express myself and falling very short of doing so, I just could not go on in this in-between state of ambivalence and confusion. It was evident to me and my superior that I did need to leave the convent.

I left in the summer of 1973, when I returned from Mexico. I had little or no emotion. My small blue trunk was packed. All that I owned was in the trunk. Some clothes, a rosary, my prayer book, a brush, a comb, and a few things like that. My navy blue purse was swung over my shoulder. In it were the six hundred dollars I was given to "get started," a Kleenex, my driver's license, and my social security card.

A few sisters came to the back door of the convent to wish me farewell and say good-bye. It was mostly a somber time now that I look back. They were losing a member of the community and, from their perspective, a very good nun and a loyal friend. My sense today is that I was letting them down by leaving them. I was no longer being a loyal religious sister.

I don't remember how I got to Mom and Dad's house, whether Mom and Dad picked me up or whether a sister drove me home. That's how devoid of feelings I was that day. Mom and Dad were happy to have their daughter home. None of us seemed to notice that a significant moment in my life was occurring and that I was unable to express either the sadness of leaving my sisters or the joy of returning home.

Mom and Dad knew that the next day I would have to drive to Marymount College, near the Los Angeles Airport, about a forty-five minute drive from our home, to finalize the process of leaving my religious community. It would involve meeting with the sister in charge of the California Province to sign papers from the Holy Father, Pope Paul VI, granting a dispensation from my vows of Poverty, Chastity and Obedience.

This was another marker day in my life—much like a day of signing divorce papers after a mostly good marriage. And again my parents and I didn't talk about it. I don't think we knew how to talk to one another. I left home at eighteen, a quiet and unemotional daughter, unable to be intimate or at ease in everyday ways like hugging, laughing, and talking about everything. I returned home very much the same.

I did feel that day. I cried all the way home from Marymount. And I talked to God on the way home in the car: *Dear God, I love you. Will I still be special now that I am not a nun? I don't want to be ordinary. Please help me to find a new way to be special. Please help me find a new job.*

I had a strange notion that after leaving the convent I wouldn't be special anymore. The church had taught me that the highest state in life really was the religious state. I wanted to be among the best, as I understood the word at that time.

As I approached our driveway, I made sure that I wasn't crying and looked all right, normal. I dabbed my eyes with my Kleenex, blew my nose, straightened my hair, and walked inside.

"How was it?" Mom asked.

I wish I had been able to tell her that it was really very hard, that I cried. That I didn't think I was going to, but I did. Sister Michael Ann was supposed to sign my papers, but she didn't show up, and someone else did it for her. Was she too sad to see me leave? I had really wanted to tell her good-bye and thank her for helping me with this decision.

But I couldn't tell my mother all that; still locked in silence and unable to let her into my heart, I simply said, "It was fine."

The next week I spent exploring jobs. Still using my coping mechanisms of detachment and denial, I moved on. As much as I welcomed a change in career, my common sense told me that education was what I knew and did best, and was the right way to go.

I was offered a job in Los Angeles as principal of a Catholic school, but I wanted out of Los Angeles and freedom from the oppressive feelings the city stirred in me. I opted for a principal position in a Catholic school in Aberdeen, Washington: St. Mary's Catholic School.

Truth is, I would have gone to Africa, Alaska, to the ends of the Earth at the time. It didn't matter that Aberdeen was a small town with a population of 17,000 and gray, overcast, and rainy most of the year. It didn't matter that Aberdeen had a higher percentage of alcoholism and suicides than most other cities in the United States. It didn't matter that I had only six hundred

Mary in Aberdeen, Washington, 1973

dollars and a suitcase of clothes to my name, that I had nowhere to live and didn't know anyone. It didn't matter that I'd never had a bank account, never budgeted, or paid bills. Mom and Dad were upset. They thought they were getting their daughter back, but she was on her way again. Maybe I was running away from something even though I didn't know what it was.

No matter what the reason for my flight, Aberdeen turned out to be a good place for me. The pastor and the sisters offered support and friendship until I could get established. The parish priest knew of a family who had an upstairs small apartment and thought perhaps they would let me rent this space. It was perfect. Small and simple, just like the bedroom I had lived in for fifteen years as a nun. I opened my first bank account at age thirty-three and wrote my first checks. Month after month I made a deposit of about $950 from my monthly salary of $1,100 for nine months of the school year. I felt rich.

I never looked back. Once I made the decision to leave the convent, the restlessness and uneasiness subsided.

19

RELATIONSHIPS

The most powerful relationship you will ever
have is the relationship with yourself.

—Steve Maraboli, *Life, the Truth and Being Free*

ADAPTING TO THE everyday things of the world came easily. The challenges of relationships did not. I had a lot of growing up to do. Intimacy remained out of reach for me. During my ten years in Aberdeen, I dated four men and had a romantic relationship with one woman in secret. Sex with men was full of anxiety and fear, and sex with women carried shame and secrecy. I was unable to experience true intimacy with either the men or the woman.

Almost immediately after settling in Aberdeen, I volunteered with a group to help youth get the support they needed to stay in school. There I met the first boyfriend. He was handsome, with beautiful blue eyes. I soon found out that he was married and separated. Our relationship was carried out in secrecy because of his marital status. Robert became my first significant male partnership. We never had intercourse because I was afraid and anytime I would reach a climax in other ways, I would cry and cry. Even I did not understand why. Robert and I led this secret, hidden affair for about two years until he changed jobs and moved away.

Soon I met Bruce, a compassionate, available, and evolved man. His full name was romantic—Bruce Castilliano. He was tall with dark hair and penetrating brown eyes. A slight smile flashed across his face when something was the slightest bit funny. It didn't matter that he was losing his hair. It made him look all the more sexy and distinguished. Mostly I was attracted to his goodness and unassuming ways. Bruce loved me and I loved him. Together we purchased a duplex. I owned and lived in one section and the other became a rental property for him—a win-win for both of us. I was proud that I managed to accomplish this investment from a starting point of six hundred dollars.

Our relationship lasted eight years, and yet I was never able to get to a level of intimacy that would lead to exhilarating sex or to marriage. I remember a time Bruce and I were attempting to make love and Bruce said in frustration, "Can you just help me out a little here?"

At the same time I was also secretly in a relationship with Anna. I felt conflict about the two relationships running side by side. Yet I stayed in each. That old coping mechanism of separating myself into pieces and compartmentalizing made it possible. I was successful in keeping others from knowing that I was in relationship with both a man and a woman at the same time. While this was something of an accomplishment, in a town as small as Aberdeen, it's nothing I am proud of remembering.

As a school principal, I was a great success. I served on the executive board for the School Department of the Archdiocese of Seattle, led retreats for the teachers, initiated a Feed the Hungry program for the homeless, and volunteered on a Family Life Committee helping youth stay in school.

Mom, Dad, brother Nick, his wife Ricki, and son Nickie came to visit me in Aberdeen. I introduced them to Bruce. He had us all over to his home overlooking the bay, which opened out into the Pacific Ocean. Bruce was a success that evening. His mild manner, good looks, and hospitality won my family's affection. He was Italian and Dad was overjoyed. Wedding bells were ringing in my dad's ears like dollar signs *ka-ching* in other people's eyes.

A friend of mine let us use his large neighborhood home

for the family visit, since he was going to be away on a business trip. Nick, Ricki, Dad, and Nickie drove from Los Angeles to Aberdeen. Mom had to fly. She was already so weak and weary that the long car trip would have been too much for her. I went to the Seattle/Tacoma airport to pick her up for the two-hour drive home to Aberdeen. I was excited. The plane arrived. Passenger after passenger filed out. After several minutes more, Mom appeared in a wheelchair accompanied by a flight attendant. My heart dropped. Mom had drunk too much on the plane. She couldn't get herself out on two feet. My excitement turned to sadness.

I wheeled Mom to the restroom. We made the silent drive home. So much silence knotted my stomach. As we neared the entrance to Aberdeen, Mom asked, "Can you stop for me to get a bottle of wine?"

I answered, "Yes, but you will have to go in yourself. I can't buy it for you." Then I prayed, *Dear God, I don't know what to do.* Tears formed in my eyes at the same time that anger flashed in them. I was mad at Mom. Then silence set in. I talked very little to Mom for the rest of the day. Maybe silence was my way to handle this trying situation, or maybe it was my way to let her know I was mad and hurt. A familiar distance that I could barely endure set in. It kept us apart—longing for each other.

I knew enough about the disease of alcoholism to know Mom desperately needed the drug to carry on. My stomach knotted up some more. We arrived at my small home and climbed up the simple flight of stairs, then sat with nothing to do but look at each other in this small space. Mom watched TV while I wondered how we lost each other and if it could have been prevented.

Soon the family arrived and Mom and I moved over to the big house with everyone. What sticks with me from that time are all the things Mom could not do with us because there was no assurance she would have access to alcohol. Each day, as the family planned outings, I was torn. Should I stay home with

Mom or go with the family? Inside I was crying for her and longing for her. The day before the family was to return to Los Angeles, she came to me, embarrassed and ashamed, and said, "Honey, I need to replace the liquor I drank from Jay's cupboard. Can you take me to the liquor store?"

The family returned to Los Angeles. It seemed to me that everyone had a great time except Mom and me. The others seemed unconscious of the loneliness and illness Mom suffered.

The summer ended but my many lives continued—school principal, community volunteer, church leader, and my life with Bruce and Anna.

I repeated patterns of unhealthy behaviors as I continued to split myself to avoid intimate sexual connections, while at the same time wanting them.

Bruce began to talk about marriage and any words I wanted to say in response got caught in my throat.

20

MOM DIES

Yes, Mother. I can see you are flawed. You have
not hidden it. That is your greatest gift to me.

—Alice Walker, *Possessing the Secret of Joy*

NOT LONG AGO, I came upon my photo of Mom with her hand cut off. I glued the photo to a piece of drawing paper and drew her right hand holding the glass of Ole Jim B back onto her body, because that was also part of Mom. The Mom I loved.

I got a call at school. It was Dad. "Your mother is in intensive care. I think you'd better come." I walked out of the school building, drove to the airport, and got on a plane. By the time I arrived at the hospital, Mom was in a hepatic coma and her lungs were failing. Her stomach rose up under the stark white blanket like the rising sun bursting into the morning.

Dad and I stayed with Mom until midnight and then we went home to rest, so I could wash my hair and be ready for the next day. But Mom wasn't there the next day. She died at 6:30 a.m. and I felt guilty that I had not stayed the night with her. I left Mom alone in the hospital in order to prepare for a day that never came. Mom passed on January 26, 1977. Mom was a young woman, from my perspective, with so much life ahead of her. She sank to the bottom and never came up. Her doctor said Mom had a death wish. I don't think so. Mom was depressed and without hope and meaning. I don't believe she really wanted to die. She just didn't know how to live anymore. And yet, I couldn't make the connection between Mom's death and my own dying parts and inability to live fully.

Mom died, January 26, 1977

There is a question we must ask over and over again of ourselves, knowing we shall die: How then shall I live?

I was still friends with many of my religious sisters from when I was in the convent, and I called upon them to help with a celebration of Mom's life. The sisters were a great help to me during this time of grief. They arranged with a priest friend to give Mom the Catholic burial we all wanted for her. Since she was not a Catholic, this usually didn't happen. Only the sisters could pull this off for me. Sad to say, neither my brother, Nick, nor my Dad, nor I were able to express to each other the multitude of feelings we held about Mom and losing her. We went to the mortuary together. I refused to participate in selecting flowers, a casket, memorial book, and other end-of-life memorabilia. I just couldn't. I shut down.

Dad placed a medallion he made from turquoise and silver around Mom's neck as she lay peacefully in her open casket. It was engraved with the inscription, "I love you."

My brother, Nick, turned to Dad and asked, "Why didn't you say this more to Mom during her life?" Dad didn't answer. His body sagged. I don't think he had an answer.

Meanwhile I, also wordless, draped a beautiful crystal rosary over my mother's hands as if to say, "I love you. You are the mother that blessed me in all the ways you knew. You are the mother I love."

After Mom's funeral in Los Angeles, I returned to Aberdeen and carried on the best I could as principal, totally immersed in the life of the Catholic Church and the community. Creating an exciting place for children to learn was a passion of mine. I did it well. It kept me engaged and allowed me to live while a part of me was dying.

Bruce was also waiting for me when I returned from California. He was still hoping for lasting love, affection, and commitment. The marriage conversation was on his mind and still not on mine. Mom's dying helped me realize that I could not go on with Bruce. I needed to let him go. I just couldn't keep holding on to a good man knowing that I would never be able to bring the depth of intimacy to this partnership that he deserved, and that we both deserved. Bruce insisted that someday our emotional-sexual connection would work. We'd had several years of fun, camping, skiing, and doing everyday things together—and it was so difficult to say good-bye.

I really did love Bruce. And he loved me. He sensed our relationship was over because of my response. Bruce sank into a deep sadness. At first I felt free and then deeply sad also. I couldn't make intimacy work and I didn't understand why. I wanted to at least make an effort to explain my feelings.

I drove over to Bruce's house one afternoon, hoping to find him and find words, to help him know that it wasn't what he did or didn't do that brought me to this decision. It was about me.

Heaviness filled the sunroom Bruce had just finished building. I sat down across from him and tried to explain.

"Bruce, I'm sorry I hurt you. I'm sorry this didn't work. I can't go on like this. I don't know why I can't be what you want and need and what I want to be for you. Something gets in my way. I can't hold you like you hold me. I can't touch you like you touch me. I am uneasy. I don't know why. This isn't fair to you and I can't do this anymore. I am so sorry."

Finally, I looked up at Bruce and tears were streaming down his cheeks. He was so beautiful to me. Silence. Silence. Finally he whispered a soft, "Thank you." More silence. The outside sun, pouring inside, began to fade into evening.

I continued to see Anna, though that relationship began to slip away too. I experienced much more anxiety than in the early phase of our relationship. Catholic guilt was having its way with me again, and secrecy was taking its toll.

My work as principal of St. Mary's school seemed complete, and the truth is, I was ready for a break. I resigned from St. Mary's in June of 1983, ending a ten-year period. Jobs were scarce in such a small town as Aberdeen, and my meager savings dwindled quickly. I couldn't keep up with my monthly mortgage payments, which had skyrocketed. Then, what I had feared happened. I literally ran out of money. Friends helped me through these trying months in order to stay afloat and not lose my home. I took various temporary jobs as an intermittent caseworker with Child Protective Services, a department store salesperson, and babysitter.

I decided to begin therapy. Esther, my therapist was young with long, black hair. She often sat Buddha-like with her legs crossed. I sat across from her in a chair. Very early into my sessions with Esther, it was evident that my Little Mary was locked inside, living in darkness and shame. She had lost her voice and lost her light of day. She was very sad and definitely left behind. The focus of our work was to reclaim Little Mary. Questions awakened the realization that Little Mary and I were strangers—miles apart. My work was to show Little Mary that I was capable of being a good parent for her now. We began to talk to each other.

"Little Mary, don't be afraid, come on out and take my hand." It was a slow process to just get us to the beginning stages of knowing that I was her parent and she was my child. She would "say" things to me like, "I'm just not sure that you love me or that you care about me. If I come out of this hiding place, will you take my hand?"

I wrote letters to Little Mary:

Dear Little Mary,

Don't be afraid. I want you to come with me. You don't need to stay there anymore—alone, afraid, confused, lonely, and frightened. I really love you. Please don't feel as if you must hide. Lift your head up. Look at me. It's all right. You are not strange. Please don't cry. I love you. I left you behind instead of walking with you. You have to talk to me and let me talk about you. Trust me. Please let me share your soul with another. As you become free, I become free. We are in this together.

Little Mary "wrote" back her confused message:

I have mixed feelings about you. Do you really want me to come out? I'll stay here if you want. I'm used to being quiet. How can I be sure that you will want me and love me? I have been away so long. Do you think I can handle the sunshine after so much darkness? Please get me out of here. Please, please, please come for me. I don't want to stay here anymore.

I began to take a parent role with her, affirming and protecting her. I explained to her what I could, yet was still not able to talk to her of rape and abuse because I had yet to come to terms with it myself. I believe this work with my child self helped to prepare me to face the truth of our abuse, but that would come later.

We relived experiences together. I took her places that she wanted to go, like the zoo and the store to buy an ice cream Drumstick—the kind with the bright vanilla ice cream, crunchy waffle cone, and the chopped nuts sprinkled on top of the thin chocolate layer. Little Mary reminded me that she didn't get an ice cream cone very often when she was young. Little Mary reminded me that when she and her brother Nickie would ride in the car with Dad, Nickie would always ask, "Dad, can we have an ice cream cone?"

Dad always countered, "If you ask for anything, the answer is no." Little Mary rarely got an ice cream cone, because her impetuous brother wouldn't, couldn't stop asking.

The day Little Mary and I ate the ice cream Drumstick was like a day in heaven. It was delicious, creamy white, and crunchy, just as we had remembered it so long ago. This day Little Mary asked and it was okay; the answer was yes. This was the beginning of building Little Mary's trust in me and of regaining her voice. We had far to go in understanding why we were split off from one another, and had barely skimmed the surface of my issues and challenges with sex and intimacy.

This was a natural stopping point for my work with Esther. Esther and I did great work with Little Mary and Little Mary and I certainly did some catching up.

Mid way into that very challenging year, a streak of good fortune happened. I received a call from the Catholic School Department of Education asking if I would accept an interim position as head mistress of Villa Academy in Seattle. It meant commuting every week from Aberdeen to Seattle—about a two-and-a-half-hour drive.

I said yes. I had to accept. No money, a mortgage to pay and a job I knew how to do were the reasons for my yes. It was tough commuting back and forth every weekend with my dog Tarsus, in the back seat. Tarsus was a very large German Shepherd-Labrador mix. He was my protector and friend.

There was something very freeing about being an interim. I found myself not worrying about ruffling feathers. If changes were needed to better the school environment or curriculum for the students, I made the changes. Truth to tell, no one seemed to mind one bit. In fact, the school board, teachers, students, and parents were longing for positive change and I knew how to deliver it. It was a win-win situation.

After finishing out the school year at Villa Academy, I interviewed for a position as principal of St. Louise Catholic School in Bellevue. I was hired. That summer of 1984, I deeded my home over to the bank in lieu of foreclosure, packed my bags, and moved to Bellevue, Washington.

The first thing I did after moving to Bellevue was to write a letter to Bruce, who was still living in Aberdeen. I desperately wanted my relationship with him to work. I longed to be normal—just marry and be a good wife. I wrote: "Dear Bruce, I am ready now to pick up where we left off. I understand myself so much better."

A gracious and kind letter followed from Bruce: "Dear Mary, Thank you for your letter. I am getting married next week."

My heart broke. I sobbed and sobbed. Looking back I am really not sure why. I think I was under the illusion I was healed and, given the opportunity, I could be normal and married to a very fine man. Everyone would be happy. My dad would be happy. He wouldn't need to ask me anymore, "What's wrong with you?"

Maybe the tears were about the deep knowledge inside me that this was not over. I was just beginning a journey of understanding who I was, the experiences that shaped me, and how to love and live within it all.

St. Louise School gave me meaning and joy in the midst of personal confusion. Over the next four years, I, along with the school community, built a dynamic learning environment.

On October 18, 1988, I was honored as a National Distinguished Principal. It's quite an honor, involving an in-depth evaluation of the accomplishments and ability to lead educational environments forward in programs and everyday service to children and families. Peers and the directors of the National Catholic Education Association select National Distinguished Principal awardees. When I received the news that I had been chosen I was excited, humbled, and grateful.

There was a send-off for me from school. Cards and good wishes filled my office. The anticipated day of the ceremony

Ms. Dispenza is welcomed home by the students at Sea Tac Airport

Mary Dispenza, National Distinguished Principal,
1988, Washington DC

arrived, and I boarded the plane along with my friend and
colleague, Janice. The few days we were in Washington, DC,
passed swiftly. I toured the White House and was led through
the Oval Office.

The awards banquet and ceremony was held on the third
evening of our five-day stay. Dressed in a beautiful, royal blue
sequined dress, I entered the ballroom. We had cocktails, dinner,
and conversation, then finally the moment arrived when it was my
turn to go forward, "…Mary Dispenza, National Distinguished
Principal, representing the United States of America." I was one

of four to receive this prestigious award. Secretary of Education Lauro F. Cavazos presented a large framed certificate of recognition to me for ensuring children a quality education. The large, old-fashioned brass school bell I was given still sits next to my desk and is a reminder of my thirty-some years in education.

Janice and I boarded the plane for home, tired and grateful. I was especially thankful to Janice for helping me with all the paper work I needed to do as part of the application process. Paper work and keyboards were not my strength. Janice knew I could use some help, and she gave it generously.

As we entered the Seattle airport after disembarking the plane, I began to hear familiar sounds. *It can't be. No, there is no way.* Yes, it was. The children. The entire school was at the airport to greet and welcome me back. I saw the flurry of red sweaters, white shirts, and students with grins as wide as the deep blue sea holding signs that read, "Welcome home," "We're Proud of You." The children began to shout, "Welcome home, Ms. Dispenza. We love you." Whistling, shouting, and clapping went on and on. Colored balloons grasped by little fingers floated in the air. It took my breath away. I was not prepared for this outpouring of love.

I was able to love children and was at ease with them. I was safe with children and I wanted them to be safe at school. They knew that I loved them, but on this day they blew me away with their loving response to me.

Amid all this wonder and adulation for me, I was carrying a personal secret. Janice, my traveling companion, and I were romantically involved. Janice was a brilliant, caring woman—a dancer, writer, and artist. She filled my need to have a close friend. We needed each other.

And the same pattern showed itself again. Before long I was dating a man named Michael as well as seeing Janice. And both these sexual relationships were devoid of intimacy and understanding.

Michael and I met at community play-acting tryouts. Michael

was a seasoned actor. I was not. I simply wanted a diversion from work and so tried out for a play and we ended up with the lead roles. Michael helped me learn my lines and one thing led to another.

I felt safe with Michael. We loved each other's company. And each in our own ways, we were lonely. When I said good-bye to Michael, his heart was not broken. We knew that our relationship was not a lifelong partnership, but simply one of convenience, fondness, support, and less-than-perfect sex. We treasured our friendship and have since kept it alive.

I resigned from St. Louise in Bellevue at the end of the school year in 1989. I am not sure what the real reason was. Perhaps I felt a sense of completion.

Just as I was ending my position at St. Louise, a friend told me of a position opening at the Chancery Department of the Archdiocese of Seattle. The Chancery was the center for all clergy affairs and various ministries serving the diocese such as prison ministry, religious education, family life, and more. The Office of the Archbishop was there also. This seemed a perfect next step for me. I was ready for a change from Catholic education and had been involved in one way or another in most of the ministries in the church.

I applied to be director of Pastoral Life Services and was invited for an interview because of my understanding of church and community and participation in various ministries at the parish level. I was chosen as the candidate to put forward for approval of the Archbishops. Archbishop Hunthausen was retiring and Archbishop Thomas Murphy was stepping into his place. Both interviewed me. They asked a question I have never forgotten.

"Mary, do you promise to never do anything that would cause shame to the Archbishops or to the Church?"

"I promise," I said. I loved my church.

I was duly appointed. Then I went home and kissed my girlfriend.

21

CHIPPING AT LIES

*Seldom, very seldom, does complete truth belong
to any human disclosure; seldom can it happen
that something is not a little disguised or a
little mistaken.*

—Jane Austen, *Emma*

WITH A PERSONAL CHANGE and a new career in the Catholic Church, I was on cloud nine. It was 1989 and I was easing into a new position that was quite a shift from my work as a principal. Yet there was a familiarity, a comfortable Catholic community of believers, and a deep commitment to service that brought me an at-home feeling.

In this sense, the Sexual Misconduct on the Part of Clergy workshop took place on an ordinary day. Just another workshop to keep us all a step ahead of the communities we were leading.

All employees in leadership positions of the Archdiocese were required to attend the workshop, sponsored by the Chancery. There were about one hundred and fifty of us gathered there. The workshop itself seemed like a good idea to me—nothing more and nothing less. Archbishops Hunthausen and Murphy knew the importance of increasing our awareness of the problem of priest abuse in the diocese. Oddly, I did not. It was never on my mind, at least not consciously.

After the box lunches, the ordinary day began to shift. The day of discussions focusing on sexual abuse somehow amplified the hidden stresses within me until a crisis point was reached.

Something shook loose. I felt as if an internal alarm was rousing me from a very deep sleep to open my eyes to the indelible secret of having been raped by a priest.

The church threw me a lifeline that day, and I grabbed it. I was still in the dark about the personal tragedy in my life, but I caught on to the challenge of holding abusers responsible, a point emphasized in the workshop. It seemed right and just.

Accountability. That is what prompted me to pick up the phone that afternoon and dial the rectory in Los Angeles looking for Father Rucker. But it was memory that then led me to TARA—Therapy and Renewal Associates for the Archdiocese—and to that circle of women spinning out their stories of abuse.

* * *

Around and around went the reels of the projector. Round and round like the circle of women I was a part of. I wanted it all to stop. But it didn't stop. The headaches lasted and the circle continued to meet. I listened to the women's stories while the pieces of my own life swirled.

It was a regular day, a school day—the day I saw him—in the darkness. I was seven years old. I didn't really know him. But I trusted him enough to sit on his lap.

Rape makes years fade together. Memory goes cold, frozen in time and space.

Remembering was now my job, the job of all the women in the circle. It was scary work because all of us had other things to do during the day—careers and jobs and the need to earn money, families and friends who worried about us. Yet we also had to remember. We had to figuratively put our minds and ourselves back in that frightening place in order to make ourselves strong enough to stand what we were learning anew as the truth of our experience.

There was magic in this circle of caring women. The circle itself enclosed us and set boundaries for us. Our circle became a sacred space that held our very secret stories and a safe place to crack them wide open. Remembering the pieces of my secret, sacred story and listening to the other women's sacred stories demanded a lot of courage, but the circle gave me strength to find it.

I eventually spun out of the circle for individual therapy, and never knew the end of the other women's stories or the real beginnings. And in order to fully open up to my own story, I needed the close and intimate connection with another person whom I could trust. Judy, my therapist, provided that.

Judy knew how to be with me. She never pushed or pulled for information. She would wait and let me experience the deep pain of my silence and the hindrance to progress it represented—not to mention the wasted session time and money. I learned to speak my feelings with Judy. I liked her short, curly hair and the way her soft eyes connected with mine.

Weekly sessions went by as I tried to uncover and recover memories. Would I confront Father Rucker? Did I really want to or need to? The question kept tugging at me.

Slowly, ever so slowly, I began to talk to Judy. No more wasting time or money. I wanted to understand and find answers to why intimate connection to another person seemed out of reach for me.

Eventually, in therapy, I decided that I needed and wanted to confront my abuser. I needed the priest who raped me to hear Little Mary. There was so much she wanted to say and needed to say. Fortified by the support of my therapist and some guidance from a friend in the Personnel office in the Chancery Department, I wrote Father Rucker a letter sharing in detail what I remembered from his abuse.

It was a long time ago, though it sometimes feels like
yesterday. The year was 1947. I was 7 years old—just a
little child. You were assisting at St. Alphonsus parish in
East Los Angeles. One day I was in the school cafeteria,
adjoining the parish auditorium. My mother, Catherine
Dispenza, was visiting with the lunchroom ladies. You
knew my mother, Catherine, well. She drove the school
bus and did some secretarial work in the rectory. Perhaps
your relationship with her brought you into contact with
me. Whatever the case maybe you took advantage of that
connection by using me for your sexual satisfaction. You
were there that day and somehow managed to get me
into the auditorium. The auditorium was dark. Rows
and rows of chairs were set up. A movie projector was
in place. You put the projector on. Then you sat me on
your lap, held me, and began to sexually abuse me. You
placed your fingers in my vagina. It seemed as if at least
fifteen minutes passed before you were finished with me.
I remember the moment you left me standing alone as
you went on your way. I was confused, alone, and afraid.
I locked myself in the parish hall bathroom. I never told
anyone. I couldn't. I was too ashamed. But now it is time
to tell and hold you accountable . . .

I also desired a face-to-face meeting, but he did not respond
directly. A serial pedophile is sophisticated in knowing ways of
protecting himself. Father Rucker had an attorney represent him,
one I'm sure he had relied on many times before. Mr. McMann,
Father Rucker's attorney in Los Angeles, wrote me back to say I
had no recourse or right to hold Father Rucker accountable. The
implication was that I didn't have a leg to stand on. It would be
my word against Father Rucker's. Surely, I would not be believed.

Unprepared for the response I received, I nearly stopped my
pursuit. Yet I was determined to move forward. My many years

of working in the church finally paid off for me, because I knew the ropes. I wrote the Vicar of Religious for the Archdiocese of Los Angeles. This person has the responsibility of ensuring that the needs and growth of priests are met and safeguarded.

After five letters back and forth, Father Thomas Curry, in charge of priest personnel for the Archdiocese of Los Angeles, wrote me a letter saying I would be hearing from Father Rucker. Never really taking any responsibility for Father Rucker's actions, he nonetheless told Father Rucker that he had better contact me. Father Rucker's attorney balked at this idea. I wrote again; this time I pulled out the trump card and said, "I really don't want to go to the media with the story of how Father Rucker molested me at age seven. I will if you make me."

That did the trick. Keeping secrets locked up is of paramount importance in a system such as the Catholic Church. The institution is committed to a code of silence and secrecy, locked as I was once locked. As long as the secret can be kept, the perpetrators go free and the church remains unscathed, not guilty. Secrecy is an unwritten code within the clerical ranks. The priests stand up for each other and create an atmosphere of secrecy, and they will stop at nothing to contain the knowledge of their sexual misconduct.

Six months after my letter, Father Rucker agreed to meet me in Seattle, face-to-face. I would have Judy, my therapist, and her colleague, Sister Francine, an expert in the field of sexuality and abuse by priests, at my side. I asked Father Rucker, by way of his attorney, for two sessions. One would take place on the first day of his three-day visit and another on the third day. The second day I reserved for processing my feelings with my therapist.

I tried to prepare for the day, but I could not. I was too distracted. A pattern returned from childhood. I could not focus. My work as director in the Chancery Department really suffered. And yet somehow I performed. I showed up, as I had as a kid, in ways that kept my colleagues from ever knowing the Attention Deficit Disorder-like behavior that was mine at that time. Silence reigned again. No one at the Chancery knew what I was doing, covering up, always covering up shameful behavior ... or behavior I thought to be shameful. Captive to the process.

I did scribble some notes. I wanted to tell Father Rucker how Little Mary felt. I wanted to ask him why I went to him that awful day. I wanted to know how often and where he raped me. I wanted to know if I was the only one, if he knew my mom, if he took me into his room. I wanted Father Rucker to know that he hurt me—my family, friends, relationships, and my ability to stay present in school. I wanted him to know how very ashamed I was. Finally, I wanted reconciliation and healing.

I never dreamed this time would come, nor where it would bring me.

22

YOUR HANDS HURT ME

*They like to use those fancy words. They
don't like to say 'raped'... They say 'misdeed,'
'inappropriate touching,' 'mistake.'*

—Charles L. Bailey Jr., *In the Shadow of the Cross*

THE DAY ARRIVED. It was a muggy, hot summer day in June of
1991, with a blue-gray sky as the backdrop for Father Rucker's
arrival at TARA. I arrived and Little Mary arrived. Judy and
Sister Francine arrived. Then Father Rucker came in.

Stand up when Father enters the room, sounded a far-away
voice like the one in my first-grade classroom or in the stage
play, "Late Night Catechism." I stood up. Did I? Maybe it was
Little Mary who stood up, as she had learned to do in Catholic
school. Stand up when Father enters the classroom. Say, "Good
morning, Father." I stood as he entered. Father Rucker reached
to shake my hand. *Shake my hand? No, I will not. How can I not?*
I felt the same boxed-in feeling that I felt on Confirmation day.
How could I shake the hand that abused me?

Your hands hurt me.

Now it was my time to stand up for Little Mary instead
of standing up for priests. Maybe this was the real beginning
of holding my child's hand and walking her into the sunshine.
Maybe this was the moment when the part of me I called Little
Mary understood that the rest of me really meant business. I
would set things right. I would set her free. It would take time

and more work, but from that day on there was no turning back.

Little Mary uttered only a few words that day. Mostly she remained locked in her very dark cellar. Father Rucker scared her back in there again. The cellar was Little Mary's place. She remembered how Aunt Annabelle had a cellar. Little Mary had watched Aunt Annabelle unlock and lock the cellar door. Often she disappeared inside. The cellar became Little Mary's hiding place.

Remembering came slowly. Then, from deep inside, a voice that I knew began to speak. Little Mary did speak.

"Did you abuse me?" she asked. She wanted to say rape, because that was what happened to her. A finger, a penis—does it really matter to a seven year old? *Invasion* is the word that comes here. Little Mary's body was assaulted, and though the scars have faded, hints of them remain.

So often I tried to remember the feelings I had the first time Father Rucker's large fingers penetrated through the tiny membrane that guarded my vagina, but I could not. Was it so shocking and painful that my body chose not to remember? Did a big wall go up instantaneously, a wall so thick that it has taken a lifetime to crumble?

"Yes," he answered to the question of abuse.

His answer didn't shock me. I wanted more.

"What did you do to me?" I asked.

"I did just what you said in the letter you sent me," said Father Rucker. He gave me no new information that day. His attorney no doubt had advised him to give no information. He was safer that way.

"Father Rucker, why did you do this to me?" Little Mary still couldn't say rape. She was too ashamed.

"I was taking hormones," he said. What a lame answer, I remember thinking at the time. I should have said it to him then.

Sister Francine wouldn't let this get by her. "Taking hormones has nothing to do with molesting children," she said.

"That's what my doctor told me," said Father Rucker.

"I find that hard to believe," responded Sister Francine.

Little Mary had more to ask. "Father Rucker, have you molested other children?"

"No, Mary, you just happened to be the little girl in the wrong place at that time."

Strangely enough, I wanted him to say something about me that made me special. I know that sounds strange, even to me. In fact it offers a specific look at the mechanism that drives away the sanity of many sexual abuse survivors. One's own inner contradictions expand shame until it covers everything inside, and the line between abuser and victim becomes blurry and thin.

I am lost in my own thoughts. My mind begins to wander. Eyes settled on Father Rucker's face. He is looking very old and tired now. Lying does that, I think. His dark brown-black hair is silver and his face has aged. We both have. He doesn't look like Superman anymore. I wonder if he remembers the little girl with braids or recalls her dimple, or did he ever really see her at all?

Judy stepped in again. "Father Rucker, it is highly unlikely that a child molester only abuses once."

Father Rucker added that he went to therapy once because he was so distressed about this one-time event. He reported that his therapist said to him, "Don't worry, the little girl will forget this and be all right and you will forget." Are there really any therapists out there who make such claims? Is there a single accredited mental health professional who would ever offer such advice to a patient? Traumatic repression is not "forgetting." I did not forget. I just didn't have the strength to actively remember for a long, long time.

Little Mary was not all right. Her conscious mind forgot

what happened but her body did not. It showed up every day in different ways, like when she wet the bed far beyond the years when it was okay and when she felt so self-conscious about not keeping herself clean. Like when she touched herself daily and bore the Catholic guilt of it all or shyly and ashamedly changed into her gym uniform. Like when her period was something she could not talk about or when she got a massive headache after each movie she saw, or couldn't pay attention in class or trust her mom and dad enough to open up to them.

Like when she learned to split.

"Did you know my mother?" I asked. I already knew he had known her because she worked in the rectory and drove the school bus. Still I should have predicted his response.

"No."

Instead of calling him out on that one, I switched topics, "Did you know me?"

"You could have been any little girl."

The truth, which he refused to speak, was that Father Rucker knew us both. He groomed me through his relationship with my mom, Catherine. "Did you rape me more than once?"

"Oh, no," he said. I didn't stop then to point out that I had specific memories of more than one occasion.

"Did you take me to your room?"

"Oh no, that would be unheard of in those days."

The rest of that session remains a blur other than that Father Rucker asked if he could give me his blessing as the day ended. But nothing was over for me yet. Because while I didn't confront him in that moment with the real answer to that question, I remained snagged by another: *Where did my flashback come from, Father—the one that awakened me like a bolt of lightning, the one that shook me to the core—the one where I was in your room and I was sitting on your lap and you were abusing me? Flashbacks don't lie I am told. Abusers do.*

I refused his offer of a "blessing." What is a blessing coming from an imposter in priest's robes? From what authority does his "blessing" flow?

"No, Father." *No. No. You will not bless me. You have no right to bless me.*

I went home after that first session with a deep sense of sadness and isolation. I was still afraid, even though I couldn't define the source of the fear. My therapist helped me immensely to process the confrontation when we met the next day.

"You don't need to sit on his lap anymore or let him rape you again," Judy said. The words weighed on me and in a strange way gave me courage to want to go back and really confront Father Rucker. Before that, I wasn't sure I wanted to see him again.

I spent the afternoon of the middle day drawing sketches of Father Rucker and writing out my thoughts for the next day's meeting. I'm an artist and have always sketched or painted my life out of darkness. My sketches of that time with Father Rucker were like sketches you see in the courtroom. They were haunting and extremely sexual. Father Rucker's eyes were riveted on my breasts. Strangely enough that is how it seemed. After sketching for a while, I prayed myself into my peaceful place and began to write.

"Dear God, help me. I am afraid. Please give me the words I need. Help me to be calm. Today I feel sick, nauseous, as if I am ready to vomit all this shit from inside. So, I listened to a priest for an hour as he told about his steroids and testosterone, which caused him to grab a little girl and molest her. So, I listened to a priest today tell me that I could have been any little girl. I just happened to be the little girl that was there at the time…Maybe this is just another day in the life of Father George Neville Rucker."

The next day I brought my writing with me. I began by saying, "I may have to read from my notes, because you took my voice away and I'm working so hard to reclaim it." After reading a few lines. I closed my folder. I spoke from a place deep inside.

What came out was Little Mary's voice. Her voice was soulful. New. Soft and low, words came out. I spoke for her as though her voice was being freed for the first time.

"I didn't want to shake your hand because your hand hurt me.

"Your name in me is detachment, disgrace, discomfort, and disconnect, depression, and dis-ease. You took Little Mary's life away. She went to school, but she could not pay attention or focus. A part of her left her body. You harmed her relationships with her dad and mom and brother, because she could not trust anymore—especially those she loved. She learned to hide. At age seven she held a great big secret inside of her ..."

Father Rucker mostly listened that day. As the session was coming to an end, Father Rucker only said, "I am sorry" and asked for forgiveness. There weren't any additional words from him, and in the end he cannily admitted only to what I specifically recalled. By the end of that second day I had no forgiveness in my heart. I only felt empty and naked and sad.

The reconciliation I desired had vanished. I didn't get the information I needed to help me understand the missing pieces of those years at St. Alphonsus School. Father Rucker lied and left me in the dark. He came and I faced him. We faced each other. That was good. He said he was sorry, for whatever that's worth when the statement is couched in lies. I wanted to hear why he was "sorry" and for what. It all felt incomplete.

"It will be a long time for me to forgive you. I want to. It will take me some time. I know that I will."

We sat in silence: Mary, Little Mary, Sister Francine, Judy, and Father George Neville Rucker.

He asked again if he could give me his blessing. I said no. Actually, it was Little Mary who said no. She had reclaimed her voice. Finally. The no was like the one she delivered to creepy Laurence when she zipped up her jacket and refused to let him go further. This time she was saying no to the dark imitation of a blessing being offered to her. The no was one of power, and came from a soul place. It came from Little Mary and me joining our voices in unison for the first time.

I realize today that claiming Little Mary's voice was the real gift that day. She had been unable to say no during those years of Father Rucker's rapes. She had been too little and too weak. And besides, he was God. Shame had bound her mouth—the world's most effective gag.

Sister Francine told me that as Father Rucker left TARA to return to Los Angeles, he turned to her and said, "This must have happened for Mary's sanctification." That comment made my stomach flip-flop. I had heard the words often in my convent days. It implies that everything that happens to us is God's will and happens for a purpose—to make us better and holier.

This was his ultimate summation of two years of rapes and their effect upon a little girl baffled by the experiences and thoroughly intimidated by his authority. After listening to me for two days, this was what he took away from it. In a single line, he offered an up-close and personal presentation of a pedophile's ability to rationalize and excuse the brutality of the harm he causes.

The next day I returned to work at the Chancery Department, frazzled and feeling that I had come to an ending of sorts, not a satisfactory one, yet with the knowledge that I had done my best. Really, I had only skimmed the surface. I did not know that my work with Father Rucker was still unfinished.

I did not know that I would meet Father Rucker again, twelve years later. And most of all, assuredly most of all, I had no way of knowing that he was on record for having raped at least thirty-three other little girls.

23

LOSING MY LIFE,
FINDING MY LIFE

If you ask me what I came to do in this world,
I, an artist, will answer you: I am here to live
out loud!

—Emile Zola, *Writers on Writing, Jon Winokur*

THE CONFRONTATION WITH Father Rucker was over, but little else was. I continued with therapy and my work at the Chancery Department, where I oversaw a department of fifteen ministries to provide resources, training, and education to parishes of the Archdiocese of Seattle. It gave me meaning and purpose.

But I had split again. By going right back to my daily routine, I acted as if facing Father Rucker had never happened. The result was that I unwittingly joined with the Chancery's environment of secrecy. I was still hiding something.

Dad was still asking when I was going to get married. The question hung in the air unanswered until I finally decided to do something about it. Friends I knew had success in meeting boyfriends through personal ads in the *Seattle Weekly*.

I began to study the ads. "Single white woman seeks warm, affectionate..." In a way, it was fun writing draft after draft and laughing through each. Finally, I liked one enough to send it to the personal section of the *Seattle Times*. Much to my surprise, I received several responses, from which I selected five to answer.

Ironically, while searching for a man, I was still romantically involved with Janice. She, not wanting to let me go, even helped me write these ads. This was mixed up, crazy. I was doing my best.

I was aware enough to see the humor in two of my dates. I received a photo from the first suitor, of a man looking great and strong from the waist up. When he arrived he was about five feet-two and alerted me to the fact that he was struggling with anorexia. The second date drove into my driveway in a gray-primed Pontiac, engine revving, exhaust pipes spewing. Shades of my past in East Los Angeles. I got into the car to find that my window would not roll up. It was stuck at half-mast and I was freezing. We headed for, of all places, Denny's. Not quite what I was expecting. My date ordered one meal for us to share. I loved the concept of sharing, just not on a first night out.

After dates with three men, I threw in the towel. I began to hate the process of wondering if I would pass or exceed or fall below the expectations of the man I dated. Never did I really believe I had as much power as the man. I just couldn't go on pretending I was having fun. I was not.

Around the time of this dating game, I was well into my second year of therapy with Judy. On her office wall hung a painting with a saying written in artistic calligraphy that ran around the outer edge of a circular image. I read and reread the words weekly, "Reality becomes the perception, the perception becomes the reality," over and over again.

During my first session, I'd said to Judy, "I just don't want to talk about women." A slight smile passed across her gentle face. I added, "Women are not an option." This was my perception and reality at the time. As director of the Pastoral Life Services for the Catholic Archdiocese, the idea of exploring a relationship with a woman was fraught with anxiety and stress.

Judy honored this request until she could no longer support my resistance. At the end of one session she offered a thought I have never forgotten: "Unless you deal with the issues of sexuality in your life, you will never know intimacy."

This thought took hold of me. It pierced my heart. It stung

and burned. I sat with it for a week. The thought of living life without an intimate loving relationship was more than I could bear. I couldn't, wouldn't spend a lifetime without a deeply loving, intimate, significant relationship. With these thoughts swirling around in me, I returned to my next therapy session and simply said, "Yes."

As simple as that, I came out. It was January 6, 1992. I was fifty-one years old. I had lived over half a century in hiding and shame. Some say "in the closet." Judy put her head down. We sat in a moment of silence, taking in the weight of "Yes," the yes that embodied the words "I love women." The words I still could not utter. Shame still held me captive. The heaviness of the moment had to do with the realization that as the director of the Pastoral Life Services Department for the Catholic Archdiocese of Seattle, living out this truth of my life was going to cause significant challenges.

Therapy freed two truths into the light of day: Father Rucker had raped me, and I loved women.

I was still making a connection for myself around truth telling. Does one truth lead to another and, if so, how? Did freeing the truth of my abuse by a priest for the first time with Judy make way for telling the truth of how I loved, and did telling the truth of how I loved make way for a deeper delving into the impact and truth of my priest abuse? My answer to that was yes.

I discovered the power of no in my session with Father Rucker by saying, "No, I will not shake your hand." Now I was discovering the power of yes. My experience suggests that telling the truth about something locked away in the past lets light into our lives, and the feeling of welcome relief carried by that light leaves us wanting more. We make a connection between our truth telling and the feeling of the light. Often the most important result of telling the truth is the courage to tell another truth. That's how it happened for me.

After the yes session, I went home and sat still with myself.

I finally rested with the truth of how I love. Soon I was done with internal thoughts and knew I needed to go outside for understanding about a community and way of living that was mostly foreign to me. I thought I didn't know another gay person at the time. That's how it is, feeling different and alone. I needed resources about living and understanding a good gay life. The first place I turned was the Resource Center in my department in the Chancery building. Why I thought I would find good information there remains a mystery to me, unless it was my erroneous and ongoing belief that the Catholic Church had the answer to everything. Predictably, there was nothing in the Resource Center other than a letter written by then-Cardinal Ratzinger, later Pope Benedict XVI, declaring homosexuality perverse and unnatural. My church clearly did not find me to be "made in the image and likeness of God."

I headed for the public library. There I knew I would find books on gay and lesbian issues and concerns. This was at the time in the early nineties when our library had just started using computers for looking up books. I walked over to an available computer, took a deep breath, and typed in the word LESBIAN. Immediately I had the sensation that the word LESBIAN was flashing in neon lights on everyone's computer. I left. I never got a book.

Next I headed for the University Book Store and slunk over to the Gay Studies section—such a strange name, as if Gay is something you study, as opposed to Gay Literature, stories to read and enjoy. I found three books: *Coming Out: An Act of Love*, by Rob Eichberg, *Amazing Grace* by Malcolm Boyd, and *The Lesbian Sex Book*, by Wendy Caster. Great books. I clutched them to my chest and went to the cashier, putting the books facedown. Because the barcode was on the back, I thought I would be spared the humiliation of seeing the line drawing of two entwined women on the pink cover of *The Lesbian Sex Book*. I was wrong. He had to turn each book over—right-side up with a slap that reverberated in my ears for a long while after. To him, I am sure, they were just more books in a long day of doing his work, but to me it was another shameful moment. However, along with the shame, I also drove home with a curious energy and excitement, qualities of feeling unmatched in my life for a long time.

I read and reflected, read and reflected, read and reflected. Like a kid tasting chocolate ice cream for the first time, I savored each word. Stories about "coming out," words I had not used before and rarely heard in my Catholic church work were becoming my words now. When I finished the book *Coming Out: An Act of Love*, I noticed that there was an extensive list of resources on the last pages. My eyes landed on a workshop called The Experience, which was designed to help persons, especially those in the process of coming out, to live lives of truth, power, and love. I picked up the phone and called for information. Amazingly, a workshop was coming to Seattle in a couple of weeks. I signed up for it. I knew, as I usually do, that this was a place that I needed to be. I was right.

On a Thursday evening in February 1992, I drove alone to the Stouffer Madison Hotel in Seattle for the opening session of the workshop. My overriding emotion was fear, coupled with excitement. I met my first out lesbian that night. Her name was Linda. I arrived early and sat on a bench, anxious for the session to begin. Linda came over and introduced herself to me. Linda understood. Several years earlier she had been where I was, feeling alone and scared. I calmed down as the dreaded time arrived. We entered together and throughout the workshop Linda was at my side.

The three-night and four-day conference began with Honey Ward, assistant to Experience founder Rob Eichberg, leading the workshop. Honey was a masterful facilitator as she challenged each of us to move deeper into the truth of our lives.

There were about seventy-five participants. I listened as each person went forward to a small platform stage and microphone, said his or her name, and what they did in life. When my turn came, legs and hands shaking, I approached the microphone.

"I am Mary Dispenza. I am the director of the Pastoral Life Services for the Catholic Archdiocese of Seattle. I just came out."

A silence followed, the kind the church causes, and then a grateful applause for coming out. In something like shock, I drove home and crawled into bed.

I was up at seven and on the freeway again for a nine o'clock start time. The day was spent in large and small group activities, each followed by an invitation to share, up front and center. After an exercise on growing up, I walked forward from my metal folding chair—oddly, it was just like the one Father Rucker sat in while he held me captive—and then I began to share.

"The fact is that when I was a seven-year-old I was raped by a priest." Again, that same familiar silence swept over the room. Church had such power over us. Church silenced many of us in its desire to keep us hidden and to cover up its many sins. I was exposing my church as I was exposing the truth of my life.

The day went on, as the next activities delved deeper and deeper into our childhood, our adulthood, our fears, and our inability to speak the truth of our lives. The last session culminated with an activity inviting us to write a letter, there on the spot, to any one or two persons in our lives from whom we still kept our coming out a secret.

I chose to write my letters to my mom, dad, and brother. The room quieted and, really, I could hear a pin drop. For a moment I felt the common oppression we had suffered, as well as the shared hope of freedom to live in the light of love. I remembered the story of a man who lived in Germany during the time in history when being gay was cause for death. The man was bold and courageous and wanted to stage a rally urging all homosexuals to come to the village square at a designated time and be out, proud and visible for one hour. As he told his plan to a friend, the friend remarked, "Why would you want to do this public demonstration and chance imprisonment for life?"

The man answered, "I would rather have a moment in the sunshine than a lifetime in darkness." That's how it was for me.

I wrote frantically. I could not get the words down on my paper fast enough. The words spilled out of me—words bottled up for half a lifetime. Tears streamed down my face. Whimpering, sniffling, and sobbing washed over the room like torrents of rain, and then a very good silence settled in. It was no longer the controlling silence imposed by the church and society. It was the calm after the storm. The silence was one of peace and the joy and freedom that result from finally, finally telling the truth.

My final sharing up front and center, in the spot where I first stood two days earlier, ended with the words, "I am Lesbian and I am proud of who I am." I got a standing ovation for these deeply heartfelt words.

I left the workshop, out and proud. Never again would I return to that place of hiding and shame. Never again! I mailed my letters to Mom and Dad:

> Dear Dad,
>
> I am a woman who is Lesbian. Please don't think of this as a failure. That would break my heart and my heart is extremely fragile right now. I don't know why I am as I am, Dad. I believe my sexuality is sacred and takes its design from the creator, God…now I can live out in truth and love and you can live with me. Thanks for giving me life, Dad. I love you.

Mom had died by this time, but I wrote her also:

> Dear Mom,
>
> All my life, Mom, I've walked around feeling different and apart—isolated and alone. I cannot live this way any longer, Mom. I must move to deeper truth and

accept the truth of who I am—a woman whose sexuality is best lived out with other women. Can you be there,
Mom, to embrace me and tell me that you love me?

In a spiritual way, I felt Mom's embrace. And Dad received
the letter with a very gracious response, "Whatever you do, I
believe in you." Yet Dad was not comfortable telling his friends.
He carried his own internal homophobia. Dad let his friends live
in the fantasy that someday I would find that prince charming
and marry. Nevertheless, Dad did stand by me and gave his very
best to something he really didn't understand.

Eventually I wrote my brother and his first wife, Margie.

I was naive to think my coming out would be all right with
family and friends. I desperately wanted to believe that they
would still love me and want me in their lives. I carried this same
naivety with me as I moved through the coming-out phase for
basically the same reasons.

Telling the truth had a cost. I was beginning to understand
another passage of scripture, Luke 9:24: "For whoever wants
to save his life will lose it, but whoever loses his life for me
will save it."

There would be more losses. Telling the truth at work would
cause me serious problems.

24

COMING OUT TO THE CHURCH

*Never be bullied into silence. Never allow
yourself to be made a victim. Accept no one's
definition of your life; define yourself.*

—Harvey Fierstein, American actor and playwright

I KNEW EVENTUALLY I would write a letter to the church and to Father Rucker. I had so much to say to both of them. But I held off and returned to my office on Monday, the day after The Experience. I felt on fire to tell my newfound truth. Nothing would stop me. I told my closest friends in the department that I had come out.

Rob Eichberg writes in his book *Coming Out: An Act of Love* that there are three phases in the coming out process—the private, the personal, and the public. An individual may choose to move through all three, or stop at the first or second phase. I chose all three. I didn't want to be simply private, coming out to only myself, or personal, coming out to only my friends. I wanted to be public, telling everyone, for I had moved to a place of pride.

This is not a good choice when you work for an Archbishop. I wanted to believe that the Archbishop would be happy that I was closer to being the image of God I was called to be. "Everything will work out," I said to myself over and over again. The church that told me I was made in the image and likeness of God would not let me down.

Colleagues responded with fear, confusion, and quizzical looks that said something like, "Why are you telling me this?"

Their reaction seemed to be, "Don't tell me and then I won't have to give this a second thought." In hindsight it was easy to see this response was in keeping with the Catholic Church and its shame around homosexuality. For some reason I didn't see it coming.

At the time, I was not in touch with how shocking this sudden coming out was to my family, friends, and colleagues. Maybe it's just as well. Had I total awareness of the complications, losses, and reactions, I would not have been able to be truthful.

Some colleagues stayed away after I told them. Father Donald, AIDS coordinator in my department, for example. I suspected that Father Donald was gay and thought he would be an ally for me. There were no allies for me, except my dear friend and administrative assistant, Joanne. She responded with joy. We had fun earlier writing drafts of letters to Father Rucker using every word rhyming with Rucker. Although we never mailed them, she loved me through it all.

Fear was everywhere. Conversations were always brief, like the one with Donald. "I attended a conference on the weekend called the Experience. I finally uncovered the truth that I am lesbian."

Donald said, "That's great, Mary. I am happy for you." I was hoping for a good conversation and understanding from Donald, but even he, a gay priest, wanted nothing to do with me after my coming out. I was too close for comfort. His comfort.

My request to see Archbishop Murphy was in motion. It was important to me to tell the Archbishop immediately. Protocol demanded it. He never responded to my request. This was strange because Archbishop Murphy had told us as leaders within the Chancery that he would always have time for us. I suspected he had heard through the grapevine about me and did not want to confront me. He knew he would let me go eventually and hoped to be spared any conversation or confrontation.

I decided I would tell my immediate supervisor, Sister Joelle. We were good friends. Having been in the convent, she was like a Reverend Mother to me—wise and formidable. We appreciated each other's qualities.

"That's fine, Mary," said Sister Joelle. "This doesn't have to be a problem. You don't have to tell anybody. We have priests and sisters who are gay and they simply live in secrecy."

"That's not good enough for me anymore," I muttered.

I left Sister Joelle's office with a pain in my stomach. Hiding the truth and living another minute in secrecy had become an impossible hurdle for me. I would not hide in secrecy and shame.

It was difficult for Sister Joelle. She and others had to make 180-degree shifts in a very short time. My colleagues were much more in touch with the reality than I was regarding the incompatibility of being a leader in the Catholic Church with openly living a gay life. Some did not want to lose me; others dropped a veil that never lifted. I remained caught between the exhilaration of finally knowing how I loved and the inevitable changes to come.

Soon after that conversation with Sister Joelle, I learned that a class was being offered at the University of Washington on lesbian and gay literature. The day I read about it was the very day of the first session. I knew that I must be there. It was too late to register, so I just went to the class. About ten others had the same idea. We stood around the periphery of the room waiting for the session to end. Finally, the teacher, Professor David Ramon, was free to ask each of us why we wanted to take the class. He was casual, brilliant, and had piercingly bright brown eyes. I told him that I had just come out and I needed to be there; I had so much catching up to do. I was selected for the one and only empty desk. It was an example of the universe getting on board with me, as it usually does, once I acknowledge what I need. David helped ease me into an understanding of and appreciation for my newly found community.

I was the mother or grandmother in the class. The students were much younger than I and were thrilled to teach me everything they knew about sex and sexuality. I learned more from them than I had ever in my lifetime. As the class was drawing to a close, a journalist from the *Seattle Times* named Lily Eng visited. Lily wanted to interview our teacher. While she was waiting to interview David, I was waiting to have the topic "Come Out, Come Out, Wherever You Are" approved for my final paper. Lily approached me and began asking me questions about the class and myself. I answered, and like any good writer, she smelled a story.

"Mary, may I do a story about you?"

"Certainly," I answered. I was done with hiding. We set up an appointment in my office, underneath the office of the Archbishop—really an "upstairs, downstairs" arrangement and probably not the most appropriate place to tell my coming-out tale. On the walls of my office hung beautiful Native American paintings, a sketch I had drawn of Mother Teresa and a framed quote by Thoreau: "If I am not I, who will be?" Lily came in with her engaging smile and friendly manner setting the stage for easy dialogue.

"What are some of the new things you have experienced since you came out?" she asked. I shared about the Timberline Tavern in Seattle, famous for its country music and line dancing. It was a large log cabin-like house with a beautiful solid oak floor and railings to lean on like tie-your-horses-up-here railings. Dancing has always been my favorite way to stay connected to my body. In dancing there was never any shame, just sheer freedom.

"At the Timberline," I told Lily as she wrote furiously to capture every word, "there are men dancing with men, women dancing with women, men dancing with women, and women dancing with men. I think heaven must be like the Timberline." I could imagine the Archbishop reading these words, which were contrary to his theological understanding of heaven.

"What does the church teach about homosexuality?"

"The church teaches that as homosexual persons, we can be who we are yet we cannot live that out." I knew I could stop here.

No. I took a deep breath and for the first time I found my voice, not my church voice, and added, "I don't believe God would gift us with our different sexualities and not want us to live those out in return. I believe that the greatest gift we can give to the Giver is to live out the gift in return."

The interview over, I left my office feeling my own private version of those famous words, "Free at last."

My statement implied that I would live out my life in whatever ways it would unfold, with or without a partner. This was just too much for the Archbishop and his understanding of what is Catholic.

When I returned from a Memorial Day weekend break, the article was out and I was out—way out. What I wanted had happened. I had shouted from the mountaintop. The headline read "Ex-Nun Comes Out of the Closet." I had not been a nun in twenty years, but the story was immediately sensationalized. I'm sure the Archbishop loved the headline.

Along with a couple of notes of affirmation, several not-so-positive responses followed. One dear friend, a mom I met at St. Louise Catholic School when I had been a principal, came to my home. She belonged to a fundamentalist church in Overlake. She knocked on the door and came in to find me standing against the hallway wall, frozen for just a moment. I knew what was coming: a castigation using passages from scripture. Before the scripture came the shame-filled question, like the one my dad asked.

"What is wrong with you?" Coming from Dad, it was simply a question about why would I not love a good and kind man like Bruce. Coming from my friend this day, it was demeaning, implying that my act of coming out was not good. It was wrong.

Then followed scripture lines reminding me that my choices were placing me on the path to hell. My friend said we could still be friends. Then she left. I remember thinking, *how can we be friends, when you think I am so bad?*

The same day I received a call from other friends who had invited me to a birthday party. The wife called to say, "Don't come." They had no longer had room for me in their circle.

Shortly thereafter a letter came from my brother's first wife,

Margie. My sister-in-law quoted scripture, passage after passage, a total of ten that she could relate to homosexuality and me. Mostly she encouraged me to turn back to God and change my wicked ways. She wondered how a "woman of God" could lose her way and now be on the path to hell. Her closing lines were: "I feel in my heart that this letter was ordered by God."

I made the assumption that Margie shared my coming out with my two nieces, Marylynn and Melinda, and my nephew, Nickie. Whatever the reason, I never heard from them. It would be years before all of us came together again. We finally realized that love trumps differences. But for a long time, we lost each other. Sad. Unnecessary.

I am grateful for my brother, his second wife, Ricki, and their daughter, Nicolle and family, for their ability to hold on to a God and a faith big enough for all of us. Without them, it is fair to say I could have lost my entire biological family. That is the real shame.

I wonder if these are necessary losses, like Judith Viorst writes about in her book by that title, or are they unnecessary losses? Viorst says necessary losses are those we all have to experience, in order to grow. In that sense my losses were necessary. At the same time, many of my losses seemed unnecessary, caused by the inability to forgive and mend fences, or the holding on to religious beliefs that have no room for loving relationships with those who are different.

The losses continued. Archbishop Thomas Murphy fired me for "breaking allegiance" with the Catholic Church. He referred to my lines in the newspaper article, "Ex-Nun Comes Out of the Closet," lines that implied that living out my life might lead to partnership and love. I had promised not to bring shame on the church. For him, this was shame.

My thirty-five-year career in Catholic education and ministry came to a screeching end. I was thrown into space like a capsule that detaches from the mother ship. I am not sure why I thought my superiors would respond differently. Denial was probably the culprit. That old familiar pattern had continued to function and kept me from facing reality.

I knew it was time to write a letter to the church just as I had written one to Dad, Mom, and brother Nick. I titled it "Fuck the Church." (Though perhaps I should have titled it "Fucked By the Church.")

Catholic schools, ministry, ritual, and community were all I really knew. Facing the truth that my life in the church was over was a dramatic change for me. The church was my home. I wrestled with the questions, "Can I stay in the church? Can I leave the church?" The tug of war raged inside me. I wrote:

> *How can I leave a church that has been the framework for my spirituality?*
>
> *How can I leave the church that has provided and been a faith community for me? How can I leave the church that has given me employment, opportunity, and meaning? How can I leave the church that has assisted me in forming values of justice, peace, and love?*
>
> *But how can I stay?*
>
> *How can I stay in a church that does not accept public challenge, especially when it relates to my life—to the essence of who I am and how I love? How can I stay in a church that upholds silence and invisibility?*
>
> *Fuck the church. If anyone is to mend this brokenness it must be I. Am I asking too much to think that I made a difference? Am I asking too much to want a colleague or friend to tell me so? Someone please ask me to come back so that I know I really once belonged. Someone please say, "Thank you," so that I know what I gave was real. Someone please say, "Your opinion matters. We want to talk about it," so that I know I was and am a part of the church. Someone please say, "The church needs you, because your experience is vital to our understanding and challenge of integrating sexuality, spirituality, and shame."*

No one can exclude me from being a part of the worshipping community and full participation in the church. It is my birthright.

Where to go? I don't know.

* * *

I was fired in June 1992. And finally, in midsummer, because of my persistence, the Archbishop agreed to meet with me. I cried and cried through my session with him. He listened as a patronizing father listens to a child, and I knew my thirty-five-year career in the church was over. Kaput.

I went to the Human Rights Department in Seattle. Their response was "We can't do anything about churches. Churches are above the law." Oh my. I realize now that this response matched well with the way churches have dealt with predators and child abuse within the priesthood. Insane.

I then sought out the canon lawyer in the Archdiocese of Seattle. There was none. He had just left to marry. Then a friend directed me to the canon lawyer of Portland. The answer and guidance I received from him was to "just be celibate." That response helped me move out of my denial and face the music. The philosophy and position of the Catholic Church and my choice to live out and proud were incompatible.

Letter writing helped me get my feelings out. It was a good thing to do. I wrote and wrote about the losses. There were many. I lost Catholicism and the Catholic Church with its liturgy and rituals. I lost community, family, friends, service, income, my career, and the way I defined myself in the world. This was the first time in my life that I understood the scriptural passage. I lost my life, indeed. All that I knew to be my life was taken away. I had to rebuild from scratch.

25

OUT AND PROUD

*If a bullet should enter my brain, let that bullet
destroy every closet door in the country.*

—Harvey Milk, *The Mayor of Castro Street: The
Life and Times of Harvey Milk*, by Randy Shilts

AT FIRST THERE WAS JOY in steeping myself in my newly found Lesbian, Gay, Bisexual, and Transgender (LGBT) community. These people were easy, fun, and real. I began to build a new community and a family of choice. I found new ways to serve as an advocate for LGBT issues and concerns. I wanted the world to be a world that celebrated all of us. So I volunteered at the Lambert House in Seattle, a drop-in center for homeless LGBT youth.

The youth were courageous and brave. Some were still in school. Many were not. Some still lived at home. Some had been thrown out of their homes for being gay. I learned quickly that the highest rate of youth suicides is among homeless LGBT youth. I gained inspiration from the courageous kids.

I joined Hands Off Washington, created in 1993 to defeat Washington State ballot initiatives 608 and 610, which threatened the civil rights of state and local public employees based on their actual or perceived orientation. I volunteered as a speaker. My own experience of being fired from my career because of my sexual orientation motivated me to do what I could to prevent this injustice from happening to others. I went to training sessions and learned the important messages to include in my

Mary works for marriage equality

speech. The initiative was defeated.

I replaced Mass on Sunday with personal prayer, long walks, and journal writing. The way I knew God and framed God had changed, but God had not. I found God in the midst of these losses to be a faithful God, just as I did when I was seven. The God I met in childhood and sustained in my soul had remained. I found meaning in telling my coming-out story at gay-friendly churches and to teachers' groups at the University of Washington. It was not unusual to be asked "Why do you need to come out?"

There was something in this question that carried shades of secrecy. Sometimes the question was framed this way: "Why do you need to tell us?" The questions bothered me. I thought hard and long to answer this question for myself so I could give an answer to others.

Coming out is about love. It is about checking out who will love me in my way of loving and being in the world and who will stand by me in this journey for equality.

To answer the questions, I wrote a poem called "Why Do I

Need to Come Out to You?" The poem satisfied me and I read it at the end of every talk I gave in support of sexual diversity. The final line is "mostly because I love you."

The sense of joy and satisfaction lasted for a couple of months and then I spiraled into a deep depression. This level of depression was new to me. Usually my involvement in work and life kept depression at bay. Now, it was here, on my doorstep, in my heart. I had little money in the bank. Beginning my paying career in the world at age thirty-three after leaving the convent was a late start, and having received no social security as a nun teaching for fifteen years in Catholic schools left me vulnerable from a money standpoint. The small severance pay I received upon being fired from my position in the Catholic Church was depleted in six months and my retirement fund dwindled. The daunting real-world challenges of having no income and no job prospects eventually wore me down.

I applied for positions in education, since my background was exceptional. Though I was always among the finalists to be interviewed, I was never selected for public school positions. All my history had been in Catholic education. I ran out of money and stopped searching for a while. I was too low in spirit. Then I took any job I could find. I became a diversity trainer and a career counselor.

Would I ever recover from this financial setback and be able to find work that matched my gifts and passion? Would I ever have a good paying job in education again? I really wasn't sure. I was so depressed. I sat around for days.

One day, in my journal, I scribbled the word *depression*. Doodling, I scrambled up the letters and found that by rearranging them I made the affirmation "I pressed on."

I interviewed for a position as the director of Prospect Enrichment Preschool serving low-income families in Seattle. It was quite a stretch for me, having no preschool experience. As I drove up for my interview, lo and behold, it was in another church building. I pulled my car up in front of Prospect Preschool. Yes, this was the right address. But where was the preschool? *Not another church. No. I won't.* I took a walk down the street to calm down.

Dear God, I can't go in. I won't go in. I can't chance another rejection. I will never work for a church again. And yet, as I finished my walk, I went toward the side door of the church building and peered through it, believing I had missed my interview. At the same moment, the interviewing team was coming out. Ready to give up on me, they were heading home. They were warm and engaging. We all went back in. We had the interview. I was hired. I learned a good lesson that day. All churches are not alike. Churches like the Prospect Congregational United Church of Christ are big enough to hold me. It was not important to the interviewing team how I loved. Instead, it was important that I was a loving person who was qualified for the job.

I remained at Prospect for eight years, and in that time I gave the families the best education and love that was in me. It was a privilege, learning more about the challenges of poverty and how families struggle and cope. The school community there was predominately African-American, a grateful, wanting-more-for-their-children kind of community. I am forever proud of my fundraising to buy a little yellow bus so that the children would have transportation to and from preschool.

The negative consequences of coming out were many, and the positive consequences were life enhancing. Through the process of coming out I experienced abandonment as well as a new and different sense of belonging and inclusion in community and love.

I can live with the consequences of love. That is the only way that makes sense to me. David Whyte in his poem, Self Portrait, writes, " *I want to know if you are willing to live, day by day, with the consequences of love...* " When it is my time to pass on and I am asked that final question—and I believe there is one—I don't think I will be asked "Whom did you love?" or "How did you love?" but simply "Did you love?" I will answer, "Yes, I did."

26

THE LOVE OF MY LIFE

This time when we kiss, I feel it in the pit of
my stomach, I feel it in my heart. And I realize
love isn't about sex. It's about connection.

--Ellen Hopkins, *Impulse*

I NEVER BELIEVED I would have the gift of intimacy and love in my life. It always seemed to be an illusion, distant and out of touch for me. When I speak of intimacy, I am referring to a romantic sexual connection to another person that is open, honest, and free from secrecy. The pattern of getting close to another, then pulling away has been with me for a long time. Coming to terms with my sexual orientation and facing priest abuse was the beginning of change.

In coming out, I never thought much about finding love. I thought more about telling the truth about my life and the freedom in that. It was later that I realized I could date and explore relationships with women without guilt or shame. This was a very new thought for me. In my earlier, confused relationships with men and women, I could not initiate any kiss, touch, or expression of intimate, romantic connection. I received. I waited, somewhat detached and fearful. Before I came to peace with my sexuality and my past, old feelings of entrapment always accompanied me to every effort of lovemaking, with a man or a woman.

After coming out, I began to date women, and the third try was a charm. It was 1993 and I fell in love instantly. It is possible. A friend I had met at a weekend workshop earlier that year invited me to a fifty's retreat she planned to attend. I was fifty-two at the time and had only been out for about seven months. I went to the retreat and as I was making my nametag, all of me sensed a woman at my side. The sensation was one of immediate connection. She was wearing a navy blue crew neck sweater over a striped blouse with perfect dark navy jeans. How preppy. I liked it. I was wearing a V-neck T-shirt over a long-sleeved body shirt and tight stretch pants that I had stuffed into my high socks. Not preppy! She had black curly hair. I had blond hair. She was tall. I was medium.

We introduced ourselves.

"Hi, I'm Mary."

"I'm Mary Ann."

I was intrigued as I watched her out of one eye. She cut a brown trunk and a scalloped round green top and placed red circles for apples on top. It was precise. Mary Ann Woodruff had made a perfect apple tree nametag. Nothing was random or out of order. My own on the other hand was wild, with splashes of color and curly bits of ribbon everywhere. It was my expression of the freedom I was feeling at the time.

The morning began with a sharing of items we brought as metaphors for our lives. Mary Ann brought a crystal, half cloudy and half clear. She shared that this was how she was feeling about her life, certain about some things and very unclear about others. She said she was struggling with a thirty-two-year marriage. My ears perked up. Maybe because the thought allowed a small window for me to squeeze through into her life, or maybe I liked her all the more, knowing she too had a struggle. When it was my turn to share, I picked up a small poster that meant a lot to me and read the printed quote, "If I am not I, who will be?" by Thoreau, and told my story about recently coming out.

The next place Mary Ann and I found each other was on the carpet, crawling to the center to pick up the objects we both brought that morning. We were face to face. Our eyes met and to me it felt as if we locked into each other's soul. Mary Ann

153

collected her cloudy crystal and I my quote and we scooted back to our places in the circle. Rita led us through another activity. She had great spiritual energy, and knew how to instill prayer and depth of thought.

Mary Ann and I met again in line for the bathroom. There, another funny moment happened as Mary Ann and I both concurred that the sharing on menopause did nothing for us. We were both beyond the days of hot flashes and happy to leave them behind.

It's fair to say that the funny stuff stopped here. As the day wore on, I wore down. The afternoon activities led me into sadness and deeper into Mary Ann. Mary Ann and I found ourselves joined as partners in an activity that involved looking ahead ten years to what it was we wanted to accomplish. We would later share the answers with the group. Mary Ann was sitting in a big stuffed leather chair, the kind in which wealthy men wearing smoking jackets relax and smoke their pipes. I was sitting on the leather footstool, where wealthy men put their feet. Our knees touched as I moved the stool closer. I began to share. I began to cry. By this time in my coming-out process, the excitement had lessened with months of job searching and my financial resources exhausted. I had just smashed my car leaving the Lambert House. The losses were indeed catching up with me. Through broken sobs, I got out the words, "I can't look years ahead; I can only look at now."

As I cried on, Mary Ann asked, "Would you like me to hold you?" *Hold me? Yes, very much*, I thought. Could I say yes? I did. I said yes. Not sure how to be held by Mary Ann in that big chair, I decided I would turn my body around and gently back up and slip myself in between her legs. Our bodies were close. Mary Ann wrapped her arms around me. Immediately, I had the feeling of being home at last, safe, warm, and connected. Sigh.

Eventually we did complete the activity. Mary Ann wanted to publish a book of haiku with photos and I wanted to have a center for the arts and spirituality. We decided that it was very possible that together we could get her book done—she, a poet, and I, a photographer. Within three days of the retreat, I received a manila envelope with all of Mary Ann's beautiful haiku. She wasted no time and I was delighted. I wasted no time and telephoned her. I invited her over for breakfast, so we could talk about the book.

Light was streaming into my small dining area, casting a beautiful glow over everything. I was so excited. The set table was a work of art. Bright orange dishes with teal edging shouted life. A small plate rested on top of each large orange plate holding a luscious yellow-red grapefruit. Little purple and yellow pansies were nestled into the center of the grapefruit. The water glasses sparkled. I sparkled with the emotion of it all. This was my seduction—my feminine joy.

Mary Ann arrived. My heart was pounding. I had not known such anticipation in my life. That very good day when Mary Ann came over for breakfast was the first day in my life that I remember being truly excited.

Everything was bathed in light that morning. Was the sun the source of that light or were we? My photographs and sketches that lined the back wall of the small galley-like kitchen caught Mary Ann's eyes. Every beautiful thing around her caught her eyes and soul. I could tell Mary Ann was home, and that she came home in this moment just as I had come home in the big leather chair snuggled in between her thighs. Mary Ann began to cry. Through her tears she uttered the word "Home." I hugged and held her. This was my turn to wrap my arms around her. The world stood still in our second embrace.

I cooked my favorite—Dutch Babies—for breakfast, with blueberries and lemon curd, a complementary, colorful delight. Mary Ann wandered into more light coming through the sunroom, calling to her. I didn't know why Mary Ann was in awe of her surroundings, but I knew I was in awe of her beauty and presence.

"Breakfast is ready, Mary Ann," I said, and we sat down together.

Conversation flowed easily across the elegant table between us. We started with the everyday questions and then deeper and deeper we went. Breakfast was slow and easy.

I remember every taste, every sight, every touch, and every sound. It was the beginning of our love for each other. I remember how we moved out of my home that day and into the back yard. Sprawled on the cool green grass we touched each other's hands softly, gazed into each other's eyes and only moved as the sun turned and finally disappeared. It is a joy to remember these moments of love and connection with clarity, unlike the fuzzy, blurry memories that take over in times of fear.

That was certainly a very good day.

We would see each other soon. We set a time to meet the following week to walk in her woods and take a photo of the cathedral she wrote about in her haiku.

Dew falls through the trees,
whispers the presence of God
in woods cathedral.

The woods were different that day. Love cast a different glow on things. Colors were sharper. Plants were greener and more luscious than I had ever seen them. I touched everything that day. Our work was to find images to illustrate Mary Ann's haikus. I found the perfect tree and the sound only a camera makes as the shutter opens and closes was music to my ears. The day was beauty and artistry. We talked and talked.

Surprising myself with my candor, I shared my story of priest abuse. Mary Ann was shocked and angry, thinking about how my church raped me as a child and raped me again by stripping me of my career and all that clothed me with meaning and purpose. She wrote another poem. She gave voice to feelings still raw and soft. She used her gift of words to speak on my behalf. I loved her for doing that.

> ...You raped me
>
> and I kept quiet.
>
> I took on the shame myself,
>
> protected you,
>
> denied my knowing that you were wrong—
>
> terribly wrong—
>
> silenced by my own child's truth,
>
> embodied your guilt, made it mine
>
> and lost my voice.

Connecting with Mary Ann that day in the forest was a continuation of the progress I had made in finding my voice. Words spilled out faster than I could think them. I told her my story.

Mary Ann told me about her children, Jim and Katie, and about her husband, Bob. She was so proud of her children. Secretly, I envied their ideal family life. Mary Ann was very proud of starting her own consulting company. Along with family and success, Mary Ann spoke of feelings of loneliness and her desire to live a life of passion and purpose. Something was shifting inside her and she wasn't sure what it was. As the morning moved into afternoon we moved deeper and deeper into the stories of each other's lives.

Over the following months, we took many walks that helped to connect her heart to mine. As we walked the forest, one season following another, the seasons of our own lives unfolded. The forest with its majestic trees, brilliant white trilliums in springtime, and crunching leaves in winter became witness to the love growing between us.

Returning from a walk through the forest one day, we found

our senses were alive. Awake. Our desire for touch and connection was palpable. Mary Ann pulled me close and wrapped her arms around me once again. Only this time, it was different. She drew me into her family den where an oil painting of red and orange hues over the fireplace combined with the red, orange and gold-speckled carpet created warmth in an otherwise cold room. She made a fire. I sat on the couch. She sat on the chair. An ottoman connected one to another and my feet rested on it. Mary Ann pulled me gently across this bridge. She reached for my hands and held them in hers. Her blue Spanish eyes darted back and forth as they did when she was serious and nervous. "I want to run my hands through your hair," she said, and she did. *Am I desired?* I wondered at her exploration and experimentation.

We talked on the phone every day and often sat on the carpet in front of the fireplace. One day sitting became a snuggle, and eventually the snuggle became a loving embrace. It happened over time. Not immediately. I welcomed her, held her tight, and we kissed so gently.

Then, from the garage adjoining the den, came a loud knock

Mary Ann and Mary in love, 2009

on the door. Two teenaged voices shouted, "Mrs. Woodruff, we came to see the sailboat!" We scrambled to our feet. I laughed and Mary Ann smoothed her rumpled clothing, pulled herself together, and went into the garage as Mrs. Woodruff.

"There it is, boys," Mrs. Woodruff said as she pointed to the small sailboat hanging from the garage ceiling. She was trying to sell it.

It felt like a close call. It scared us. What were we doing? We decided we would not go forward. We stopped communication for a few days. After about a week we thought it would be all right to talk on the phone. But in spite of our good intentions, we found ourselves returning over and over again to each other.

27

BLACK BEADS

Patiently I wait,
Like the silent blue heron,
longing for the catch.

—*Waiting*, Mary Dispenza

SOMEWHERE ALONG THE WAY, Mary Ann told Bob, her husband, about our relationship.

Mary Ann had yet to work through her marriage and bring it to closure in a way that honored all that it had been. When Mary Ann and Bob divorced, my role became one of loving support as Mary Ann's grief and loss over her divorce entered our partnership. Our love sustained us, but of course I longed for the moment when we really could move on in freedom and love.

Dad came to visit me for my birthday on May 22, 1995, two years after I met Mary Ann. That's when he first met the love of my life. Mary Ann and Dad got along extremely well. After everyone went home that evening, Dad, Mary Ann, and I stayed up talking and laughing the night away. Dad caved in first and we all happily said good-night.

Finally alone, Mary Ann and I grabbed some blankets and tiptoed outside to that grassy place where we'd spent the first day together. But now we watched the moon instead of the sun and we touched instead of talked. Under the blankets on a starlit night, our bodies met. Moonstruck and caught in its spell, we said, "I love you."

Mary Ann awakened very early in an attempt to leave before

Dad knew she'd spent the night. She tiptoed into the house and there was Dad, at the round oak table, doing his usual morning crossword puzzle. He looked up at Mary Ann, smiled and said, "Good morning, Mary Ann." No more secrets here.

Dad remained a true friend as well as a loving father. When many left me, Dad stood by me, reminding me over and over again that he believed in me.

Dad and I were finally getting to know each other. He flew to Washington many times and never missed a Christmas with me after Mom died. I smile when I recall Dad helping me wrap T-shirts for the Lambert House Youth Christmas gift bags. The shirts had different gay logos and sayings printed on them. He held up a black tank top with white lettering on it for me to see as a half-quizzical smile slowly made its way across his beautiful Italian face. The question printed on the shirt read "Pretty Queer, Huh?" I kept that shirt. I have worn it to every Pride Parade in Seattle since, in memory of that day when Dad and I were truly connected.

Dad remained a private man, never really showing the depth of his pain or joy to me. And yet, I knew by the time Dad died that he really cared about me and that he was very proud of me. It has always been hard to acknowledge that in my earlier years Mom, Dad, and I were strangers.

In June 1995, upon returning home from my birthday visit, Dad was diagnosed with thrombosis and liver cancer. He was a strong eighty-three by all outward appearances, but the prognosis wasn't good.

The doctor said over the phone, "Mary, the best thing you can do for your Dad is to get here and be with him." I flew to Los Angeles and Dad and I spent the last month of his life together. My brother just could not do this for Dad. His deeply vulnerable heart would not let him. I went through scrapbooks with Dad and we talked about beautiful memories together. Thank God for photos that hold memories when we cannot. We tried to play cards but his attention wandered. One day, knowing his love for music, I asked, "Dad would you like to hear some music?"

"Yes," he said, nodding.

"Which CD, Dad?"

He whispered in a weakened voice with a soft beautiful smile on his face as he raised his bowed head and looked up at me. "Patsy Cline."

I grew more and more in love with Dad and with Mary Ann, who joined me for a week to help care for my father. She held me at night and comforted me by day. Dad knew how we loved each other and that made him happy. One night I let Dad sleep through his medication time. He was so tired. He awakened very early that morning, crying out for me. I ran to his bedside. Mary Ann followed. Dad was shaking and freezing cold. I believed he was going through withdrawals from his medicine. Eight hours had passed since I last gave Dad his medication. My intuition guided me. I laid my body on top of Dad and Mary Ann somehow wrapped her body around ours. Circle of peace. The warmth of our bodies penetrated his, and Dad's shakes subsided. A loving embrace brought Dad the calm he needed. Then I gave Dad his medicine and he soon leveled out. When Mary Ann returned home I missed her terribly.

Dad and I said good-bye to each of his faculties, one by one—his hearing, the light in his pale blue eyes, and the smile on his loving face—until finally he said, "Good-bye." Dad died July 13, 1995, a few months after meeting Mary Ann. And for the first time in my life I had someone to comfort me in my grief and hold me close, Mary Ann.

Thank God that after losing Mom, Dad knew what he must do before he passed on: come home to himself, his son, and his daughter. His grandchildren visited during his illness, especially Nicolle, Nick's daughter by his second wife, Ricki. Nicolle loved her grandpa so much and was such a help to me. Marylynn and Melinda, Dad's grandchildren from Nick's first wife, Margie, visited Dad and asked me to read a card to their grandpa. The card asked him to turn his heart over to Jesus, so that they might be together with Jesus in heaven. Being fundamentalist Christians they held to the belief that unless Dad did this with intention and fervor, he would not reap the rewards of heaven. Dad knew God and loved God. His heart belonged to God. And he knew putting on a show for them was not necessary.

I believe that Mom and Dad are together now in an everlasting embrace. Maybe that is God, since God is love. No more separation. The unending intimacy and love they craved is finally theirs.

And my longing for the same came to an end during the fifth year of my loving relationship with Mary Ann. The moment arrived that I had feared—the moment when the patient great blue heron must act. I was the blue heron, waiting, watching, and longing for the catch. There was no movement in our relationship. I had always told myself that when we came to this place of no more growth or movement between us, I would stop and let Mary Ann go.

We were away for a weekend in a cozy cabin on Puget Sound. I said to Mary Ann at the end of another loving day, "Mary Ann, we're stuck. I need to let you go now. Until you find yourself, you will not find me. If you do and I am here, we can move on in our love for each other. That is my hope." We agreed to separate, pure and simple.

I wanted Mary Ann so much that my heart ached at the thought of losing her and yet at this point I did not have her. We did not have each other. Mary Ann spent the next month in silence, praying and writing. I spent the next month alone, nursing a broken heart, crying, writing, and feeling very lonely. Those were days of anguish and pain deep inside. I understood heartache from that breakup. The love, connection, and intimacy I experienced with Mary Ann were pure gifts. I did not want to lose her. I really questioned whether I would lead a meaningful life without her. I fought off old feelings of abandonment. Was I simply being used?

28

FINDING YOU—
FINDING ME

*You've got to find yourself first. Everything
else'll follow.*

—Charles de Lint, *Dreams Underfoot*

A MONTH SEEMED LIKE a thousand years without speaking to each other. Every time I thought of Mary Ann, familiar waves of sexual energy washed over me and I felt like I'd been left on the shore. I kept active in the community and continued volunteering at the Lambert House. In spite of the activity, never a day passed that my heart did not ache. Then one day when I returned home, I found a note on my door from Mary Ann. It simply said, "Yes!" Of course, I wanted the yes to mean "I love you and I want to be with you." It did not. It meant something more important. Mary Ann had found herself as a woman whose deep love and affection is best expressed and lived out with a woman. I had always said to Mary Ann, "Unless you find yourself, you will never find me."

I knew the power of her yes having said my own yes, much earlier.

Finally our separation ended. We met. We embraced. We walked the Fauntleroy Park near Puget Sound in Seattle, where gentle pathways hug the bay on one side and a bluff of grassy meadows and fields rise up to greet the sky on the other. As we walked, story after story poured out of Mary Ann, telling me about her journey to this point—this moment of living out—and yes, this moment of being sure she was in love with me.

My position as director of Prospect Enrichment Preschool helped me get back on my feet. I was regaining my confidence and belief in myself. Mary Ann was doing the same. We were spending as much time as we possibly could together. Mary Ann, still a little shaky from her divorce, would only move in with me if we saw this coupling as a test. I named it "The Great Experiment."

After six months together, I passed the test. We knew there were no further reasons to stay apart. Life together was easy, fun, romantic, and real. How blessed I was to be able to crawl into bed at night and wake up in the morning next to the woman I loved. I smiled every morning when Mary Ann would look over at me from her side of the bed. One morning she said with all sincerity, "You look like a movie star." I melted.

Two years after The Great Experiment, we bought our own home together. The process frightened Mary Ann. She feared discrimination. She purchased our home as a single woman and joint ownership papers followed later. I, on the other hand, was still in the "Let's shout it from the mountaintop" phase. Unbeknownst to us at the time, our home's former owner, Melanie, had a sister who is a lesbian and she was the one who had remodeled our new kitchen. We were in the backyard with Melanie one day, thinking we had disguised our partnership, when Melanie exclaimed in a voice that would have wakened the entire neighborhood, "Wait until I tell my sister that we sold our house to two lesbians!" Aargh!

After Melanie left, I picked Mary Ann up and carried her over our threshold. That's an exaggeration. The truth is I picked up one of her legs and set it over the threshold.

Perhaps one of the most romantic moments we have shared together was an evening right after the closing on our home. We had not moved in yet. It was Mary Ann's birthday, June 6, 2000. I invited her out for a special dinner.

That was the pretense under which I lured her into the most

romantic evening of our lives. We were dressed up and both looked stunning. We liked doing that for each other. On the way to dinner, I said, "Mary Ann, I want to drop this extension cord off at our new home." I added that Rich, our handyman, needed it.

The cord was a ruse, of course. My heart was pounding again. Would she be surprised? Would this be the evening of romance and love I anticipated? Would this be a birthday she would always remember—perhaps among the best? I wanted that for her and for us.

We drove up our driveway with pride. I asked Mary Ann to come in with me. "Let's see what Rich has been doing." Mary Ann was eager to sneak another peek at our new home. We'd just started up the winding stairs to the threshold where I had lifted Mary Ann when we heard beautiful chamber music. Was it Bach, Beethoven? Feelings of love and excitement surged through me as the music drew us into our sunlit living room still bright in the Pacific Northwest summer evening. Dramatic, sheer curtains flowed from ceiling to floor at the windows that encircled the room. Two musicians, a violinist and cellist, played for us—only for us, the music resounding from the cathedral ceilings.

"Happy birthday, Mary Ann." I said. "We are home."

Coming from the kitchen were delicious aromas. A gourmet chef had prepared dinner for us. I'd borrowed a card table and two folding chairs, candles, and a white tablecloth and set them up earlier that day. In the emptiness, just a table set for two. Candlelight. Champagne. Yellow roses. That table, in that space, at that time, meant more to us than any other. It was our place and our time.

I'd brought our sleeping bags. We spent the night in our beautiful new home. Yes, yes, and yes! It was a very good day and the beginning of the continuous music of our lives together. A new ode to joy. It was the end of some things and the beginning of others.

Last summer when I was walking on the beach with Kurt, our seven-year-old grandson, I picked up a stick and drew a huge heart in the sand. He stood by watching me, Mimi, as I am called, scribble in the heart, "Mimi + --------" and before I could get the next word down, he exclaimed with delight, "Grandma!"

Some very good day, when Washington State allows everyone who loves each other to marry, Mary Ann and I will marry and our grand niece and nephew, Alli and Logan; our grandchildren, Tess, Jamie, Rita and Kurt; and our family and friends will scream and shout, dance, and cheer. Then everyone, especially the children, will have words to put with our partnership—words they understand: married. Until then I will work with others to bring marriage equality to Washington State, believing that, as one group rises, so do we all.

Mary Ann and Mary stand for marriage equality

29

THE PEARL OF GREAT PRICE

*This pearl has become my soul ... If I give it up,
I shall lose my soul.*

—John Steinbeck, *The Pearl*

SOME RITUALS ARE worth keeping. Some are not. My time in the convent had given me a grounding tradition known as the Spiritual Exercises of St. Ignatius of Loyola, prayers and meditations developed by St. Ignatius to help people deepen their relationship with God. I continued this yearly practice after I left the convent. Each summer, I found a place where I could have silence and an environment that supported prayer and reflection. Often I landed at my friend's cabin in Sequim, Washington.

I often built my personal retreats around a theme. "Soul Bowl" was the theme one year. It provided a framework for me to search for what fed my soul. The summer of 2002, I chose the theme of gratitude and called my retreat "The Pearl of Great Price." Mary Ann and I were living together and deeply in love. I was happily employed and I had finally faced Father Rucker.

It was time to thank everyone in my life who helped me arrive at this place of gratitude. The goal I set for myself was to actually write a letter of gratitude to the giver of the "pearl" in each case. One after another, I remembered pearls I cherished. As I thought about my spiritual life as a gift, my mind traveled back some forty-five years ago to that small bathroom where I began my conversation with God. That small bathroom was where I went for refuge from my rape. Like the waters of Baptism, I washed and washed my sullied body. God was there in the horror of it all, letting the free will of each of us have its way. I never asked *Why, God?* My God was not a God who allowed or did not allow this priest to rape me. God was there in the midst of it. God loved me. The thought gave me comfort.

How does one thank another for doing harm, even if one of the identified outcomes is as good as a deep spiritual connection to God? You don't. At least, that was my decision. Instead I decided to write Father Rucker a final letter of closure and forgiveness. I wanted to think I was done with Father Rucker and that this chapter of my life was complete.

On a yellow tablet dated July 25, 2002, I wrote:

> …It is more beneficial to me to close this
> chapter of my life and reach for complete healing,
> forgiveness, gratitude, and love. My childhood
> rape by you was a great loss of innocence and the
> ability to connect to self and others. The pearl in
> this tragedy was the beginning of a lifelong spiritual
> journey with God.

I mailed this note to Corpus Christi Church, in Palisades, California, where I knew Father Rucker had been assistant pastor and then appointed as pastor in 1979.

Much to my surprise, two weeks later, I received a letter from Monsignor Craig Cox, the Vicar for Clergy for the Archdiocese of Los Angeles, saying my note had been forwarded to Father Rucker. The Vicar wrote that earlier that year, "Father Rucker was removed from all assignments and agreed to change his residence to a retirement facility where he is monitored by the chaplain and director who know the essence of his history. He has been prohibited from all public ministry." He added that there was "currently a police investigation of Father Rucker," and he gave me a number to call if I wished to provide any information about my own experiences to the police.

I was stunned by this news. An inner voice talked to me. *You're finished. You're done. Move on.* Then another soft voice, my own, whispered, "What if there is another woman in Los Angeles who could use some support?" That voice won out.

I dialed the number. I asked to speak to someone about abuse by a priest. The woman who answered directed my call to the detective in charge of the case. I was shocked to realize that Father Rucker was counted among the criminal sex offenders of Los Angeles.

When Detective James Brown answered, I told him in a fumbling and bumbling style, a little about my story.

"Mary," said Detective Brown, "Father Rucker is a bad, bad man. He has hurt many children, more than I can tell you." Did I hear the word *many*? Wasn't I the only one? No, Father Rucker was on record for having molested and raped dozens of little girls. Brown had been documenting Father Rucker's history and, because of my phone call, he now had evidence to place Rucker's history of child sexual abuse as having started as soon as he became a priest.

Father Rucker had been moved from parish to parish, starting in 1951, when he was transferred from St. Alphonsus School. Detective Brown could track these moves, as family after family reported Father Rucker to the police department, or went to the bishop or pastor about their child being abused by him. Detective Brown was determined to bring Father Rucker to justice.

The Catholic Church knowingly allowed Father Rucker to have continued access and opportunity to prey upon children, while covering up his growing record of abuse. He was transferred from parish school to parish school, always having access to children and young girls. His role as the parish priest and pastor gave him the power he needed to remove girls from the classroom without any questions asked by the nuns who taught. No one at the local level was above the parish priest.

In 1979 Rucker had been rewarded with an appointment as pastor of Corpus Christi Parish in Pacific Palisades. Why on earth would a Bishop appoint a serial pedophile priest to the rank of pastor, a leadership position in the Catholic Church? Cardinals James Francis McIntyre (1947-1970), Timothy Manning (1970-1985), and Roger Mahony (1985-2011) appointed guilty priests like Rucker to position after position. They failed the church miserably in not removing pedophiles from the priesthood as their offensive behaviors came to light. Detective Brown told me how frustrated he was because the Cardinal denied him access to the records necessary to prove that Father Rucker had an ongoing pattern of raping and abusing children.

Father Rucker was indeed a serial pedophile. At the end my first phone conversation with Detective Brown, he asked me to come to Los Angeles to meet with him and the District Attorney's representative. He also gave me the name of an attorney, John Manly, in the event that I wanted to pursue a personal case against Father Rucker.

Los Angeles made my stomach ache. It made my eyes water and I couldn't breathe very well. For years I went there only to see family and friends. But now I was summoned there for something far less appealing.

Mary Ann and I boarded a plane to Los Angeles and arrived at LAX, a busy airport filled with bustling humanity coming and going. We took the shuttle from the airport to pick up our rental economy car from Hertz. A lovely lady with rich dark skin, stylish glasses, and a marvelous smile helped us. Out of the blue she offered us, at no extra charge, a beautiful red convertible for a very sunny day.

I recoiled. *No. Flashy. I can't have flashy today. This is a somber day at the Los Angeles Police Department.* Later we kicked ourselves and said that was exactly the day to have driven a flashy red convertible.

Our first stop was to see my brother Nick in Torrance,

California. In his younger days, Nick was an Elvis Presley looka-like. My high school girlfriends still ask, "How is your handsome brother?" Nick had taken early retirement from an exceptional career at McDonnell Douglas Aircraft. A senior supervisor who had worked his way up the corporate ladder without losing his soul to the workplace, he lost it instead to drugs and alcohol. We had a brother and sister connection as deep as the deepest ocean. I loved him beyond words.

Now Nick had a small antique shop called Nick's Pieces of the Past. Nick was unable to support or comfort me. This didn't stop my wanting it.

I hammered on the screen door to the shop, hoping for Nick to answer. He peered out of the dark, depressed interior. He looked at me, really looked at me.

"You're so pretty. Are you my sister?" he asked, half jokingly.

"Yes, Nick, I am."

"How did you get so pretty?"

Was Nick seeing me for the first time? I didn't know. Mary Ann stood there, stunned. We three walked out of his small shop, through the alley and into a barrio restaurant where we had the best huevos rancheros imaginable—a good part of Los Angeles.

Now it was time to go meet Detective Brown. As we approached the Los Angeles Police Department my heart was pounding and my stomach jittery, like it was full of bumblebees. My insides were playing their own interlude of flight and fear. Detective Brown. Detective Brown. The name played over and over again in my mind as if I might forget it.

Several minutes later we entered an office crammed with stacks of paper. Detective Brown and his team had been dedicated to the case against the Los Angeles Catholic Church for years. Child-hood abuse by priests hung like a heavy cloud on a dark, dark day in reports pinned to the wall, in the words rolling out of mouths, in scribbles on the notepad by the phone, in recently clipped arti-cles from the *Los Angeles Times* pinned to the corkboard. Sexual predators seemed to lurk in every corner of that room.

"Hello, I'm Mary Dispenza and this is my partner Mary Ann. I'm here to see Detective Brown."

"Oh hi, I'm Teresa. I'll tell Detective Brown you are here."

We waited. The bumblebee still buzzed inside me. We made small talk. Mary Ann asked questions. Teresa was friendly, young, and willing to talk to us. She gave us a sense of the problem—unending abuse and rape by priests, collusion on the part of the church to keep this quiet—but told us very little about Father Rucker. Then Detective Brown entered the room. He was good looking, both strong and gentle in his appearance. We shook hands and, in a matter of minutes, he, Teresa and I walked to a small, sterile room to meet with Deputy District Attorney Christina Fleming of the Sex Crimes Division. Mary Ann waited and read through the material about abuse by priests, statistics on abuse in Los Angeles. A *Los Angeles Times Sunday Magazine* cover that featured Cardinal Mahony lifting up his dress to display the Cathedral where his genitals ought to be made her smile. We both got an education that day.

The room was poorly lit and felt confining. There were four of us around a small table with folding chairs: Deputy DA Fleming, Detective Brown, Teresa, and me. We were together in that room for two hours.

I swore to tell the truth.

"Please start at the beginning, from birth forward."

I did. I talked about childhood, my mom working in the rectory, Rucker's abuse, the convent, the impact of it all, fear, shame, coming out, being fired, healing, therapy, my struggle for intimacy, and more.

"I can't believe you were a nun," said Christina. *What do nuns look like?* I wondered. I think Christina said this to lighten the heaviness that took over that very small room. I felt oppressed, weighed down by shame. We weren't done. Detective Brown asked the million-dollar question:

"Mary, how would you feel about talking to Father Rucker on the phone, while I tape you? I think it would work because you just sent a card to him and you will be on his mind. The call will have a context. It won't be out of the blue."

My stomach dropped. My ethics kicked in.

Like Watergate, I thought. *Isn't that against the law? That's not fair. But rape is unfair to children. This is a very bad, bad man we are talking about…*

Undone by anxiety, I left my body for a moment.

Finally, I shared my fears and asked, "Can you frame this for me in a way that makes it just and the right thing to do?"

Detective Brown smiled. "There was a thirteen-year-old boy who was raped by his father when the boy visited him on weekends. It was the boy's word against his father's. The boy agreed to a taped phone call between his dad and himself. It was the phone call and what was said between them that gave the boy the edge. The father was found guilty of abuse and rape and so was held accountable. It was the taped phone call that saved the boy."

The story helped me see the taping of my conversation with Father Rucker in a better light.

"All right, what will I say?"

Detective Brown told me not to worry; we would go through it together and he would be right by my side. But I did worry.

Swirling and twirling, I am lost.

As our conversation came to an end, Detective Brown told me the date had been set for Father Rucker's criminal trial. I would return to testify.

Detective Brown told Mary Ann and me to take a forty-five minute break. We had the same idea: a visit to the multi-million dollar Cathedral for Our Lady of the Angels, the mother church of the diocese and church of Cardinal Mahony. It was a short walk from the police department. As we were admiring the inside sanctuary of the cathedral, we were abruptly interrupted by a gentleman saying, "Everyone will have to clear out now. His Eminence is going to have his photo taken." This whole thing made us laugh. Just a half hour ago I was telling my story about a pedophile priest under Cardinal Mahony's watch, and here we were now about to watch Cardinal Mahony have a photo shoot for his great cathedral.

We returned to the LAPD and I went directly to the taping room. A dark, cleared desktop stared up at me. Detective Brown directed me to the chair behind it, sat me down, and put a small black tape recorder next to me.

He plugged in the phone and listened to the dial tone. It was loud through the speakers, so very loud, piercing the wall I'd built around myself to detach from the implications of the call. We practiced. He pretended to dial. We pretended Father Rucker answered. I sat in stillness, heart pounding, and a mixture of right and wrong running over me. I wasn't sure my voice would work. I wasn't sure Little Mary could do it, or even if we should do it. The wall crumbled and rebuilt, crumbled and rebuilt. Eventually, Detective Brown and I were ready. He dialed the number and handed me the phone.

Father Rucker answered. Detective Brown fed me questions. But fear crept in. I was so afraid. My heart hammered in my throat. I was there and yet I was not. Ordinary greetings rolled out of me into Father Rucker's lap and into the hands that raped me.

"Hello, Father Rucker. This is Mary."

"Oh yes, Mary, I am happy to hear from you. I got your note." He was referring to the closure note I had written him recently. The one about ending this chapter of my life.

"Father Rucker, can I ask you some questions?"

"Yes, Mary."

"Remember when you did that to me. Did you do that to other little girls, also?"

"Yes, Mary. But only on top of the clothing."

Detective Brown shoved scrawled questions in front of me and I continued to ask each of Father Rucker. Father Rucker in his aging, faraway voice answered:

"Yes, Mary."

"No, Mary."

"I don't remember, Mary."

"Bingo!" Detective Brown said softly in the background. Bingo! Bingo! Father Rucker had given an answer Brown needed.

"Am I done now?" asked a voice inside me. *"Please, please."* The words of a poem I'd written long ago came rushing in—

> I cry.
>
> You do not hear tears fall gently
>
> within sheltered walls,
>
> keeping old wounds alive and moist.
>
> They are there, aching, throbbing,
>
> longing to hear outstretched
>
> hands say I love you.
>
> I cry, can you hear me?

The call ended. Detective Brown had his Bingo.

If only we had chosen the flashy red convertible and could have driven off into the sunset right then. Father Rucker's answer, "Only on top of the clothing, Mary," gave Mary Ann and me the comic relief we needed for the rest of our time in Los Angeles and then some. This was not the end—just more information. There would be more games to play. I would return.

30

A TWIST OF FATE

*Salvation for a race, a nation, or class must
come from within. Freedom is never granted;
it is won. Justice is never given; it is extracted.*

—*A. Philip Randolph*, spokesperson for African-
American rights in the 1940s and the 1950s.

IT TOOK TIME for me to decide whether or not I would call John
Manly, the attorney contact given to me by Detective Brown.
How could I not, when I learned more about the number of
women's lives damaged by Father Rucker's criminal behavior?

When I made the call to John, I was at preschool. The sun
was streaming through the third-floor window of my small office.
Photos of children, beautiful children, hung on the mustard
colored walls. I'd turned it into a warm, creative, loving space.
I felt at home in it. It was a great place from which to make a
very scary phone call.

Closing my office door, I was flooded with feelings of shame
and secrecy. I didn't want anyone to hear me. It was an unrealistic
concern because no one was there to hear me. The phone rang
and the same feelings returned. Fear. Shame. Anxiety.

"Manly Maguire Associates. May I help you?"

"May I please speak to John Manly?"

"May I ask what this is regarding?"

No, no you can't, I wanted to say. Instead I said, "It's about
priest abuse."

John came to the phone and asked if his colleague, Patrick Wall could join in. I liked them both instantly. There was a genuine quality to their voices and our conversation. John Manly was warm, compassionate, and smart. Patrick Wall was spiritual and steeped in an understanding of Catholicism, patriarchy, the power and secrecy of the Catholic Church, as well as abuse by priests. Together, John and Patrick were a formidable team.

My story poured out, never before told in such depth. They encouraged me to tell it all and took the time to listen to everything. I went on and on for about an hour and a half.

"And then he..." My voice faded into silence. Into that detached place so familiar to me. In and out I went. They encouraged and supported me in every sentence.

"There are so many young women who are unable to speak up and out about the terrible abuse they suffered," John said.

I understood. As I had been at my coming out, I was ready to stop living in secrecy and shame. I was ready to speak.

Mary Ann and I took another trip to Los Angeles in the summer of 2003, this time to Costa Mesa to meet with John Manly and Patrick Wall in person. I wanted to see them face-to-face. I needed to have a connection beyond the telephone and e-mail. Their office space was extremely professional and spoke of success. First I saw and was introduced to Patrick, who looked like a linebacker from Notre Dame, and then John Manly entered the room. He was warm and down to earth. And would you believe it, there in John Manly's office was a leather chair like the one where Mary Ann first held me—a comforting thought and feeling.

Once again we three shared stories—mine about Father Rucker, theirs filling in the gaps of what little I knew about his history and about the history of the Catholic Church's cover-up of priests' sexual abuse. Patrick had been a Benedictine monk and canon lawyer, whose job was to mend fences when his brothers had abused little children. When he could stand it no longer, he left his order and became a lawyer, joining John's practice and bringing to it his knowledge of canon law. Ryan DiMaria was another of John's associates. His high school principal, a pedophile priest, had molested him for years. Ryan was the recipient in 1997 of $5.2 million, the largest settlement that had ever been made between the church and one of its victims. Ryan used part of his settlement money to become a lawyer. He and John were both motivated to heal victims, hold "perps," as they called priest abusers, accountable, and save and heal the church they loved.

John explained the Window of Opportunity to me. In July 2002, the Window Law was passed and signed into effect by Governor Gray Davis of California. This law gave a one-year window of opportunity, during 2003, for lawsuits alleging sexual abuse by priests to be put forward. Over 800 lawsuits resulted. An estimated 500 were connected to Los Angeles. Mine could become one of them.

It was at this time that I learned the shocking truth. Father George Neville Rucker, a serial pedophile, was accused of molesting thirty-three girls over five decades. That number, of course, can only represent those who came forward and can never reveal how many more were effectively betrayed, shamed, and silenced by the church on his behalf. He was perhaps the worst perpetrator on record. Over the years I had never asked myself if there were other little girls being raped and abused by Father Rucker. Now I knew there had been.

Yet, at some crazy, mixed-up level, I felt sorry for Father Rucker. By this time he had grown old, too old to punish, I thought. It would be a while until I could sort out all my feelings.

John Manly's comment about the many young women too ashamed and afraid to speak out about their abuse had a great impact on me. Perhaps John was right; they could use my voice.

Ultimately I said yes to John. More importantly, I said yes to my own healing and to giving my inner child an opportunity to heal and speak her shame. I moved forward and became part of both the criminal case and a civil case pending against George Neville Rucker and the church.

On June 3, 2003, a civil case was filed on my behalf in the Superior Court of the State of California. Jane DM Doe versus John Doe 1, a corporation sole; John Doe 2, a corporation sole; John Doe 3, an individual; and Does 4–100, inclusive Defendants. I didn't quite understand this verbiage back then. They were just words. I never liked being Jane Doe. I asked to be named, Mary Catherine Dispenza, because that is my name. Too long had I remained invisible. No more secrets, I told myself. But the lawyers explained that this was how it was done. I learned as the case proceeded that John Doe 1 was the Roman Catholic Archbishop of Los Angeles, Cardinal Roger Mahony; Doe 2 was St. Alphonsus Church; Doe 3 was George Neville Rucker; and Doe 4 was St. Alphonsus School.

In the case stamped number BC296810, fourteen complaints followed: Childhood Sexual Abuse, Assault, Battery, Intentional Infliction of Emotional Distress, Fraud (Concealment), on and on to Negligent Supervision and Negligence. Sixty-one pages later, John Manly, attorney for plaintiff Jane DM Doe, Mary Catherine Dispenza, signed the Complaint.

Ryan came to Seattle and did "interrogatories" with me. Question after question was asked of me, both orally and also in writing. It was exhausting.

Meanwhile, Detective Brown's criminal case against Father Rucker was proceeding. In a ploy to escape trial, Father Rucker set off on a two-month cruise. Detective Brown was determined to have Father Rucker taken to trial. He tracked him down, boarded a helicopter, intercepted the cruise ship near the Aleutian Islands in Alaska, and had it diverted to Dutch Harbor, where Father Rucker was plucked from the ship.

A *New York Times* article on July 13, 2003, even reported on it: "Alaska state troopers arrested him, harnessed him on a tug boat and returned him to Los Angeles, where he faced charges of molesting 12 girls over thirty years, starting a year after he was ordained as a priest in 1946. If convicted, he faced a possible prison sentence of 26 years."

In May 2003, I received a subpoena to appear on July 7 in Los Angeles Superior Court as a witness in the criminal case: *People of the State of California v. Rucker, George Neville.* I was to appear at 8:30 a.m. in the courtroom of Los Angeles Criminal Division, Department 504. The subpoena was a scary piece of paper. It seemed so official with square boxes everywhere stating important things like "NOTICE: Immediately upon receipt call witness coordinator." And, "Disobedience to this subpoena may be punishable as contempt of the court (Penal Code Sec. 1331)." The only lighthearted part about this piece of paper was a funny little hand stamped on it with one pointing finger to the very important box about special instructions. It made me smile, this attempt to ensure that I would really look at the very important box. I had never seen a subpoena before. I needn't have worried about it.

The terrible irony in the criminal case against Father Rucker is this: Father Rucker walked into the Los Angeles County Superior Court facing life in prison for allegedly molesting twelve girls and walked out a free man. In an article "Charges Dismissed Against Priest," which appeared in the *Los Angeles Times* July 8, 2003, Richard Winston wrote: "Prosecutors dropped the charges in the wake of a U.S. Supreme Court decision that struck down California's effort to prosecute molesters in older cases."

The Supreme Court ruled that victims could not prosecute sex offenders retrospectively if the offense took place outside the California State statute of limitations that were in place at the time of the original crime.

The day had nearly arrived for justice, and then it was gone. I wondered how everyone working on these cases felt. Detective Brown had put years into tracking Father Rucker's crimes of rape and molestation against little girls. We had all done our work.

I was disappointed with this turn of events also. I had decided to have my time in court and give my voice to all the women molested by Father George Neville Rucker. I wanted to tell and show everyone that repressed memories are real and that the trauma and effects of childhood abuse are lasting. I wanted to tell the world how the Catholic Church failed children.

I received a letter from Steve Cooley, Los Angeles County District Attorney, by way of Christina Fleming, the Deputy District Attorney (Sex Crimes Division). It read:

> As you know, the United States Supreme Court
> recently ruled in the Stogner case that Penal Code
> section 803(g) is unconstitutional in the way that it
> was applied in certain cases. The case in which you
> were a victim has been affected by the ruling. Our
> office wanted to formally inform you that further
> legal action took place that resulted in all charges
> against Mr. Rucker being dismissed.

My attorneys were quick to reassure me that victims would not be forgotten. Ryan DiMaria wrote:

> …The fact that the criminal case was ruled
> unconstitutional does not have any impact on the
> civil case statute of limitations. The good news is
> that your CIVIL CASE is proceeding and being
> worked on every day.

Steve and Ryan ended their letters much the same:

> …Our office remains concerned about you and the
> effect of this case. If you have any questions… Our
> office is committed to assisting you and obtaining
> justice for victims of child sexual abuse.

31

THE UNBROKEN SILENCE

*Child abuse casts a shadow the length of a
lifetime.*

—Herbert Ward, director (1970-2000) of
St. Jude's Ranch for Children, Boulder City, NV

THREE YEARS AFTER my deposition at the LAPD regarding the
criminal case of Father Rucker, my attorney, John Manly asked
me to be present at the deposition of Father George Neville
Rucker for the civil suit being filed against him and the church.
It was now 2006 and we were at the Los Angeles Sheraton, in
the ballroom of all places. I arrived at the Sheraton the evening
before the deposition, alone and frightened. Heart pounding.
Once in my room, sleeping was difficult. I finally fell asleep
after a couple of restless hours, only to be awakened by the three
rings of the wake-up call. It was about 8:00 a.m. when I arrived
in the ballroom. No one was there. Mary Ann, an organization
development consultant, was leading a retreat and could not be
with me. I wanted her by my side.

Down the room's center were about six long tables connected
to one another and chairs lined on each side. There would be no
dancing in this ballroom today, except for Father Rucker who
would soon be dancing around answers while his attorney took
the lead. My mind wandered, as it can when I am threatened, to
the Seattle Hilton ballroom where I dance and perform simple
routines with my Arthur Murray dancing teacher, Ross. Dancing connects me to my body. It brings me such joy. How can a

ballroom be turned into this—this mockery? A ballroom is for dancing, not for depositions. The ballroom was cold. The joy was gone. I was cold. I found a place at the table and put my folder down. My stomach did a flip-flop. I headed for the door. I needed to get out of that ballroom. As I left, *he* came in.

I saw Father Rucker enter from the other end of the ballroom. He walked in with a cane, wearing a powder-blue sweater and black pants—still a nice looking man with silver-white hair. He took the first seat at the left-hand side of the head of the table across from where the convener would sit. He stared across the table toward the wall. I glanced at him and quickly turned away. *I don't need to stay here*, I told myself and made my way out.

As I left the ballroom, another victim was entering. She noticed that I was upset. She gave me a hug. She said, "I'm going to sit across from him and look the bastard in the eyes." She was strong and angry. In that moment, she gave me her strength. I proceeded up the escalator as my attorneys, John Manly and Ryan DiMaria, were going down. They smiled encouragement to me as we exchanged hellos.

I wandered around the lobby for a while, then went back down the escalator to the ballroom. Now I saw it as an auditorium of sorts. I flashed to the auditorium of long ago. The one I still see so vividly. The chair I sat in now had that same cold feeling of long ago. A priest in a chair, only this time he sat alone—no one on his lap.

I sat alone dressed in my new red jacket and black pants. My chosen power suit for the day. I was not feeling powerful. Little Mary felt that familiar feeling of abandonment and fear. But now we were at least together, my child-self and my woman-self. I took a deep breath and thought, *you will be sitting in* my *lap today, beautiful little girl.*

My new friend, Terry, leaned over and whispered that Father Rucker used to corner her after church on Sundays and rub up against her, always watching her. The kids at the Catholic school dubbed him "Rub-a-Dub Rucker," because he would touch the girls as they passed him in line to and from church. Shocking. It's difficult to believe that no one in authority seemed to know about or be willing to prevent this abuse.

The attorneys representing each of Father Rucker's victims had a turn in questioning him. No wonder we had to meet in a ballroom. The enormity of his pedophilia registered within me. Mary was not alone. In a most horrible way, she had dozens of sisters who understood her pain.

John Manly had his turn to question Father Rucker. Father Rucker was accompanied not by one, but by three attorneys. Such power has the Catholic Church. Money. Money makes the church go around. Parishioners would stop putting money in the Sunday collection baskets if they knew that this was where much of it is headed.

The attorneys were in their power suits also—dressed to kill. They advised Father Rucker not to answer any question of importance. I found it quite interesting that Father Rucker could name several seminarians in his class from some fifty years ago, yet could not remember raping or molesting anyone in the room. The deposition led nowhere, except back to secrecy. Secrecy again prevailed. The church prevailed. Father Rucker prevailed.

Mr. Steier, Father Rucker's lead attorney, set the rules. No question would be answered that might possibly incriminate Father Rucker. Well, then, basically Father Rucker answered nothing. The following excerpts of that day in the ballroom are taken from my notes, from Bishop Accountability.org and from the City of Angels Blog post, "Father Rucker, What Are You Hiding by Invoking the Fifth Amendment Over and Over Again?" (September 1, 2009).

In a very low voice, head and eyes cast down, Father Rucker replied over and over again, "I assert my right to remain silent and decline to answer that question."

After endless questioning and no answers, my attorney John Manly grew frustrated and said:

Just for the record, I want to make it very clear, I
am not done. I think the Archdiocese once again,
just for the record, I think there's a pattern and
practice of basically making people travel a long way
with absolutely no intention of having them give a
deposition. And I think you set the date. You knew
this was going to happen. It's wrong.

It was wrong. It was all wrong. It ought not be happening.
Yet, it was happening.

The questioning continued. John Manly was relentless. He
plowed ahead. He was unstoppable.

MR. MANLY: Father Rucker, isn't it true that you
abused children when you were a seminarian?

MR. STEIER: I'm going to instruct my client not
to answer that question for the fifth, the sixth, the
right of privacy.

John continued to ask a series of questions that demonstrated
a pattern of Father Rucker being moved from parish to parish
while all the time the Archbishops were aware of Father Rucker's
continual and devastating sexual abuse of children.

MR. MANLY: Were you assigned to
predominantly African-American and Hispanic
parishes because you were an abuser?

I hated that question. St. Alphonsus Catholic School, where
I was raped, served predominantly Hispanic families. Hispanic
Catholic families most often love their priests. A priest can
do only "good" in their eyes. Priest abusers' protective armor is
reinforced by the admiration of the Hispanic people. The priest

was God. The hidden implication in this question appalled me, as did the fact that it was true—the church used and abused its members.

> MR.MANLY: Did you ever receive telephone calls from Cardinal McIntyre about complaints?

> MR.MANLY: Is it true that the Archdiocese knew you were an abuser of children before you were ordained?

> MR.MANLY: Isn't it true, Father Rucker, that it was not a secret while Archbishop Levada was serving in the Archdiocese that you were a child molester?

> MR. MANLY: Did Monsignor Hawks ever talk to you about allegations that you had abused children?

Question after question received the same answer from Father Rucker.

Father Rucker finally mastered his lines, "I assert my right to be silent," was his response over and over again.

He did not need to be prodded by his attorney, who announced with pride, "My client now doesn't need me to instruct him anymore. He's beginning to get it."

With that, my attorney, in exasperation and cynical humor responded, "How good for you." I laughed. It struck me funny that Father Rucker was getting it, *it* meaning how to respond correctly. I wondered—was he getting the message of the magnitude of his offenses and the depth of the pain and scars left on his victims? I didn't see anything on his part that made me think so.

And finally, questions that jarred me and caused my memory to float back to my childhood.

MR. MANLY: So Father, isn't it true that Father O'Dowd was pastor at St. Alphonsus School in Los Angeles while you were an associate there?

MR. STEIER: I'll instruct him not to answer.

MR. MANLY: So, Father, isn't it true that when Father O'Dowd was pastor at St. Alphonsus that he repeatedly told you to stop touching children and molesting children?

MR. STEIR: I'll instruct my client not to answer …"

MR. MANLY: Isn't it true that Father O'Dowd reported you to the Archdiocese?

MR. STEIR: I'll instruct my client …"

MR. MANLY: Isn't it true that Father O'Dowd was well aware that you were abusing girls at St. Alphonsus in Los Angeles while you were an associate there?

MR. STEIER: I will instruct my client …"

MR. MANLY: Did Mother Liguori talk to Father O'Dowd about Father Rucker?

The names Father O'Dowd and Mother Ligouri awakened resting memories of that time so long ago. I saw each of them, including my mother, parade before me, as if I were seeing a rerun of a movie. New questions flitted by on the screen. Did Mother Ligouri know of my abuse? Sounds like she tried to do something about it. That was good news to me, because I loved the sisters.

Did Father O'Dowd know I was being molested? Was my mom aware of this concern on the part of Father O'Dowd, for whom she worked? Father O'Dowd, from my childish impression, was good and kind as the pastor of St. Alphonsus. He was round and mild-mannered with soft blue eyes. Irish. Not all priests are bad.

The deposition went on and on. Toward the end, my attorney, John Manly, said that he wasn't done. He had more questions to ask of Father Rucker.

MR. MANLY: Father Rucker, do you recognize the woman in the red jacket near the end of the table?

FATHER RUCKER: No.

This was one of the very few yes or no answers Father Rucker gave in the entire deposition.

MR. MANLY: She is Mary Dispenza. Is it true that you put your fingers into Mary Dispenza's vagina?

FATHER RUCKER: I assert my right...

MR. MANLY: Is it true that you raped Mary Dispenza?

FATHER RUCKER. I assert my right...

MR. MANLY: Is it true that you knew her mother, Catherine Dispenza, who drove the school bus and worked in the rectory for you?

FATHER RUCKER: I assert my right...

No answer, no answer, no answer. "I assert my right...I assert my right...I assert my right..."

The questions continued. The attorneys for both sides bantered back and forth. Always the same response from Father Rucker's attorney, "I am going to instruct my client not to answer that question."

I sat there thinking how useless this was. At the same time it was the first time someone was sticking up for me. It was the first time I heard the words said out loud, "Did you rape Mary Dispenza?" No more secrets for me. That was one of the gifts of this day of exposure.

The next attorney took the chair in front of the microphone and began to interrogate Father Rucker.

> Is it true, Father Rucker, that you stood outside
> church and as the lines of girls passed by you lifted
> their skirts?
>
> Is it true that the upper grade students at St.
> Monica's named you Rub-a-dub Rucker?

"No," was the word Father Rucker answered over and over again. His attorney continued to jump in with, "I cannot allow my client to …"

Suddenly Jana, another victim and Terry's friend, left the room. Father Rucker used to take her behind the altar and rape her. He told her she was special in God's eyes. As Jana left the room, I noticed that her friend quickly followed. I noticed that my attorney followed Terry. Something inside of me said, *You need to be with Jana and Terry. We are victims and survivors and we need each other.* I got up and followed.

There, on the carpet, leaning against the wall like a heap of broken, bruised bodies, were my new friends. Two women like me, scarred by Father Rucker. Jana was crying and shaking fiercely. Terry held Jana as John Manly encouraged her to breathe. He said to Jana again and again, "You will be all right. You are safe." In that moment I loved my attorney. In that moment I knew that John cared. He wasn't only my attorney. John was a compassionate man.

I observed, close up, the terrible wreckage of women's lives caused by childhood priest sexual abuse. Terry asked Jana, still shaky, "Where are your meds?" She looked up and said with a faint smile, "We all have meds, don't we?" I froze. Everything stopped. I wondered, *am I that wreckage?* In that moment the wreckage and I were one. We were all one. I could not separate myself from them.

Wreckage. I don't know how many times I was raped, or how frequently, by Father Rucker. Father Rucker molested me from the second through the fourth grade, age seven through nine. That, I've been told by my attorneys, was his mode of operation. Where? In the auditorium, behind the school stage, in his bedroom? God knows. As I look at serious accidents and see only the wreckage, I say, "Wow, that must have been a terrible accident." Sometimes there is just a heap of pieces, like the women on the carpet that day, to tell us about the damage. I know the extent of damage in my life, the cost and work of healing the wreckage. Immense, significant wreckage. Sometimes wreckage is caused by accident. Sexual abuse of children is not an accident.

I met a young man that day also. He was lost and alone. He believed himself to be the only little boy that Father Rucker molested. He said he thought Father Rucker sought him out because he "was cute and had long blond curly hair."

My heart sank to realize that as far back as 1947, a good priest, Father Patrick O'Dowd, tried to alert Cardinal McIntyre that his associate priest was touching and molesting children. Father Rucker was not removed from positions where he had access to children. Instead he was passed on and on, from parish to parish, to rape and abuse, rape and abuse, over and over again. Finally in 2002, Father George Neville was defrocked. Fifty-five years. That's a very long time to shelter a pedophile priest. Maybe I am wrong, yet I believe the action was taken for the same reasons it was withheld—scandal and fear.

> *Dear God, I think I've had enough. This day has*
> *exhausted me. I hate this ballroom. I'm getting sad*
> *watching Terry and Jana shake. My own body is falling*
> *behind. I'm going to have to catch it up, God, somehow.*

The church protects pedophile priests in an effort to prevent scandal. The church only defrocked Father Rucker at age eighty-two because he was becoming too big a threat to the Catholic Church's image and pocket book. Removing him from the priest-hood was not about protecting children. The church could have and should have done that, years before. It was about not wanting to get caught with their pants down. Father Rucker's history of abuse was becoming a liability. A big one.

Scandal, fear, and the potential of financial settlements, rather than a desire for truth, justice, and healing were the culprits behind every answer left unaddressed by Father Rucker and his attorney. This kind of response made attaining justice very difficult.

It is fear that motivates the church to cover everything up and hide the truth. Richard Sipe, a former priest and a leader in the area of priest sex abuse, addressing SNAP (Survivors Network of those Abused by Priests) victims/survivors in 2013, offered this thought: "The institution that cannot tell the truth about itself has nothing to say." The church is a wrongdoer that believes it must maintain its image at all costs. Revealing the true evil of priest sex abusers and the cover-up would bring everything the church says and teaches into question. The Cardinals rationalize that if the truth were known, the church might die and then the legitimate good they do might cease. Every totalitarian society shares this view of itself. Necessary evils, these things are called. Actively protecting the evil things done to us was necessary, *so the church could go on doing good work…*

32

THE WALLS CAME TUMBLING

The wound is the place where the light enters you.
—Rumi, *The Book of Rumi*, Coleman Barks

MY BODY WAS getting left behind. I really hadn't thought much about it. Wherever I went, it always followed. I usually focused on my soul and had plenty of thoughts going on. But my body was getting very tired. Wearing down. It never really occurred to me that besides my soul, my body itself was also desperately seeking peace from Father Rucker's abuse.

Things were slowing down regarding the case, also. Moving into the third year of this trying process, I wondered if there ever would be justice.

I believed that our experiences have a major impact on our bodies and knew better than not to care for myself. But in spite of that, I left my body unattended. Things that my soul longed to say and release were embedded in my body, to its detriment.

My neck had been hurting and pulling a little to the right. It was relentless as it ached and pulled throughout the day. Preschool work became more and more tedious—especially sitting at the computer for hours. My body still wanted its turn to speak and be heard.

Finally, I went to a wise physical therapist, who sent me to a neurologist, Dr. Chang. The examination seemed simple enough. I could stick out my tongue, close my eyes, and touch my nose with my right index finger and then with my left. The walk down the hallway was a breeze and yet my head was visibly being pulled to the right and I was in pain.

The tip of my tongue curved to the right and my right arm did not swing when I walked down the hallway. I don't know what else Dr. Chang observed that day. He wanted me to have a CAT scan to check out my brain.

The year was 2005. That year gripped me like a vise, a tourniquet. I cried every day. Twisting tighter and tighter, I didn't understand what was happening to my body.

"Mary Ann, the doctor said this pulling and pain I'm having might be the beginning of Parkinson's. He's not sure. He is going to do some tests."

Mary Ann held me as she had in that big leather chair where I first encountered her strong embrace. She whispered softly, "We'll get through this, whatever it is."

Mary Ann wanted to know everything the doctor said. She loves details. I like the big picture. The details were few. The big picture was that I was in pain and my neck hurt. I had the CAT scan and the findings showed that I had a "grossly normal brain." That was excellent news, in spite of sounding peculiar. Mary Ann and I were relieved, yet still fearful of the unknown. My diagnosis was made on the basis of movement—the pulling muscles and the slight twisting of my head and neck.

This was the same year I hoped my connection to my attorneys, the priest, the church, and Cardinal Mahony would end. End. Ended.

My case was about to be settled, I thought. But I was terribly unsettled. I eventually learned that something called cervical dystonia was attacking the tonal quality of my neck muscles. It's a painful neurological condition. My brain sends messages to the nerves of my neck, causing my neck muscles to contract involuntarily, making my head twist to one side and drop somewhat to my right shoulder.

It was like being in an all-day workout with myself. Being pulled one way, then another, I struggled to stand straight. An involuntary pull to the right, while I pulled back to center, became an all day fight. Exhausted by this tug-o-war, I often fell asleep on the sofa, dead in a deep slumber induced by clonazepam, a benzoid drug.

Dystonia had its way with me. My head began to pull more to the right. It was impossible to get comfortable or straight. There was no position, other than resting flat on my back, that brought comfort. Comfort was a gift, I quickly realized.

I also realized that my body might be paying the price for years of holding secrets. Maybe this was some of the "pain and suffering" attorneys often mention as a part of a settlement.

Mornings were the toughest. I would crawl out of bed, wondering where I'd gone. Totally knocked off my feet and my body still wanting to tell me something, I awakened each morning in sadness, not gratitude. This new development frightened me.

One day when making coffee I reached to fill the carrier for ground espresso beans when the gripping, pulling, twisting pain started. The pain was unbearable and paralyzed me. Like one of the four unfinished Prisoners by Michelangelo, I was trapped by muscles that felt like stone. And like those half-chiseled figures, I was fighting to free myself. The prisoners were captive and unfinished in the stone. I wanted to be free and finished. My body had more to say.

Mary Ann heard the click of the espresso machine and came to me knowing the morning pain my body experienced. She gave me a hug, rubbed my shoulder, smiled.

"Can I do anything?"

"Thank you," I said, "I'm OK."

Coffee. Tears. One tear, always out of my right eye, would slowly tiptoe down my cheek. I would grab the back of my neck with my left hand and straighten my head up, up. The daily tug-o-war began. With my free hand I pounded the grounds deeper and deeper into the carrier and lost myself in the sounds of the Rancilio Rocky coffee grinder. Next destination: my brown leather chair, my resting place, my praying place, my writing place, and my healing place. In daily journal entries, I documented my body's journey to health and wholeness.

So many questions came rushing in: Was it my fault? Was it something genetic that caused my dystonia? Was it that hard fall at aikido practice? Was it scrubbing chapel floors and white-tiled convent porches for too many years, or was it the twisting inside trying to get free from Father Rucker's raping hands and body? Was it the sadness in me? Was it living in secrecy and shame all these years? Was it the holding pattern of some forty-five years? Was it from the slight curvature of my spine that I've had since I was a child? Was it the stress and intensity of the past three years given to finding Father Rucker guilty for his sins that caused the twisting and pulling in me? When I was working for the Archdiocese, without fail I could count on my shoulder locking up every few months. Frozen. The pain always started in the middle of the night, so intense that I would get up, drive myself to the emergency room at Group Health Cooperative. They gave me a cortisone shot into my frozen shoulder and pills for pain and inflammation. I would drive back home, crawl into bed, get some sleep, wake up in a couple of hours, and drive to work at the Chancery Department.

A positive outcome of being fired from my position as director of the Pastoral Life Services for the Catholic Archdiocese was that I never had that frozen shoulder again. Bodies do talk. Mine did. Freed from the frozen shoulder and the church to some degree, I wasn't expecting another round with Father Rucker, or this second round with body talk. This was a crazy-making time for me. In the time just before my case settled, my body had its turn to really fall apart. I was mad at everyone, including the neurologist, Dr. Chang. Maybe he was right. Maybe I was a psychological mess at the time. I formed a healing team and brought them all to Dr. Chang's office. Looking back, I realize that four women in a tiny examining room was overkill. Then, I thought it was the best way to get through this new territory. Finally I asked for pain medication. For eight months I took clonazepam.

To offset the negative energy, I also took a trip to Africa in celebration of completing forty-five years in education. I retired from Prospect Enrichment Preschool, and Mary Ann and I planned a five-week adventure to Africa as volunteers with an organization called Cross-Cultural Solutions. We both hoped my case would be settled soon after we returned. Mary Ann, my faithful partner, was always there for me and endured, along with me, the ups and downs of my quest for healing. So many times I connected with her and then pulled away. Because of her love and her ability to stay with me through the in-and-out times, my trust in relationships grew.

The compound where we stayed in Tanzania was in a small town called Moshi, at the base of Kilimanjaro. We loved our time and work in Africa, and felt the challenges of it. Every morning I walked with two other young women to the Majengo Clinic nearby. I loved being greeted by the children.

"*Shikamoo.*" A Swahili greeting of respect for older persons.

"*Marahaba!*" was my response, meaning, "Thank you for your respectful greeting."

The Majengo Clinic supported the health of pregnant women, babies, and persons living with and dying from AIDS. My main work was to weigh babies and record their weight, then ask the mothers:

"*Anashida?*" Do you want to see a doctor?

The babies either screamed or looked bewildered as they stared up at me, the *shikamoo*—the older respected white woman. White was sometimes the scary part. I may have been the first human being the little ones had ever seen with such odd-looking pale skin.

I learned how to count in Swahili so I could tell the parents their children's weight. Every day I would fill in weight graph cards for each child. The cards were small and the graphing section filled with tiny squares. My hands shook uncontrollably as I meticulously placed the small dots for graphing the baby's weight on the blue soft cardboard card. The medication I was taking made me shaky. It was embarrassing.

Finally, the doctor in the AIDS clinic trusted me enough to do AIDS testing, something I really wanted to do. It involved placing drops of different chemicals on tiny squares to make a positive or negative reading. I tried. The kind doctor took his strong dark hand and wrapped it around my trembling white hand to hold it steady. A moment, a precious moment when a white woman from America and a black man from Africa wanted nothing more than to help each other. As much as I wanted to do AIDS testing, I could not. I just shook too much. The clonazepam made me too shaky and fuzzy.

The daily bout with pain was changing me. When I returned from Africa, my body, mind, and spirit seemed broken. My body still battled to reconcile spirituality, sexuality, and shame. From my convent life I had drawn the gift of meditation. Each day I meditated. One morning after clearing my mind, a beautiful, pulsating purple light appeared before my closed eyes. I began calling it my God light.

I never questioned the science of it. What mattered to me was that it was calming, beautiful, and a gift from sitting and waiting in silence. The purple light returns from time to time in prayer and meditation. My God light.

My experience in Africa made me realize that I had to pursue approaches other than clonazepam to deal with my recurrent pulled muscles. I read about Botox injections. Still I was afraid and did not want needles poked into me or the poison of Botox in my system. Yet I knew I needed to try it, because it was the only known help to minimize pain and stop the symptomatic pulling of muscles caused by dystonia. The strongest motivating force was the possibility that I might be able to stop taking drugs.

The date was set. I went. I took my blouse off and put on the white, flowery, softly laundered gown and climbed on the stark white table.

33

BODY, MIND, AND SOUL UNITE

> *When we touch the place in our lives where*
> *sexuality and spirituality come together, we*
> *touch our wholeness and the fullness of our*
> *power and at the same time our connection*
> *with a power larger than ourselves.*
>
> —Judith Plaskow, *Standing Again at Sinai:*
> *Judaism from a Feminist Perspective*

DR. MESCHER EXAMINED ME, asking me to close my eyes and let my head do what it would while I thought of a happy place. He observed the tilt of my head. He left to get the small needle, filled with the slightest amount of Botox. Behind the table sat a machine that looked much like a TV. The doctor's nurse attached cables from the machine to the pulling area of my body. This helped Dr. Mescher know if he was in the vicinity of the spasm-wracked muscles. The machine would make an "I gotcha" sort of sound as static noises crashed together when the needle connected with the right muscles. Zigzag lines traveled across the screen like bolts of lightning, giving the doctor another way to observe how close his needle was to the spot to be treated. Before the doctor could get a needle near me I dissolved into a puddle of tears—uncontrollable tears.

I wasn't prepared for my own traumatic response. Nobody was. I tried so hard to unravel my feelings. My therapist, Deborah, a brilliant, compassionate woman with ash blond hair and a beautiful smile, listened to my fears and we practiced an imagery activity to get me through my next appointment. Deborah knew me well, having worked with me through the past five years. My guided imagery took me to a happy place. My happy place ended up being a place Deborah, Mary Ann, and I were all familiar with. It was an estuary off the beach at San Pancho, Nayarit, Mexico. It looked like a beautiful, small island with lush plants, exotic vines, and magnificent trees. *Pajaritos*, birds, were everywhere. Egrets, white and stately, and little tiny birds, chirping, squawking, diving, gliding, landing, and taking off. The sandy ground, the thick jungle, the edge of the water, this place represented freedom.

Another month passed and then my scheduled appointment arrived. This time I was ready. I had prepared by way of creative imagery, meditation, writing, and talking to my therapist and friends. My fears had diminished. I still cried every morning and my head and neck remained extremely pulled and twisted to the right. It hurt.

I did it. I put on my hospital gown; Mary Ann tied it in the back. Dr. Mescher said, "Close your eyes and think of something happy." While my eyes were closed, he assessed the pulling and decided where to put the injections. He left and returned with a vial of Botox. I sat on the edge of the table and grounded myself. I hugged the pillow to my breast and closed my eyes and went to the estuary, saw the beautiful birds, heard the water sounds. The four injections caused my body to jerk and a couple of tears dropped down my cheek. It was done. The process was over in a flash. That was the good part, and such a little blip in the scheme of life. Looking back, I believe my body held so much for so long that finally it tightened up and said No more, please. Then it twisted up and unwound itself, doing its own work of releasing.

Every three months I was scheduled for my Botox injections, and every three months I struggled with the process. I considered the pluses and minuses of Botox for pain and to address the symptoms of my pulling muscles. I still had an aversion to medicine and medication. My wonderful body healer, Dr. Joyce Hawkes, knew that I was struggling with taking medication and encouraged me to say a prayer while I was receiving the Botox injections. Dear God, help my body take in only what it needs and let go of the rest. The prayer helped. It was a reminder that medicine is good, that I needed help, and that my body had the power of rejecting what it did not need.

The Botox did minimize the pulling and the pain. And without pain, I began to enjoy walks and life again. I continued to bless the Botox again and again as I encouraged my body to take the good from it and throw the rest away. I added alternative helps such as dancing, meditation, and yoga to the use of Botox.

Mary Ann and I faced the changes and challenges together. We both realized how much give-and-take partnership asks and how very important we are to each other.

"We will get through this together," Mary Ann said at the onset, and we did.

This spiritual journey gave me the needed permission to cry me a river, to rest, unwind, and heal. It pulled me deep inside where so much shame resided, into the swamplands. And deep in that swamp, energy and life lived also. In the murkiness of it, the twists and pulls of it, I found a coming together of my body, mind, and soul.

I am on a learning curve, piecing my understanding of health factors together with my childhood trauma of sexual abuse. I knew that priest sexual abuse is usually kept a secret by the perpetrator and the victim and often goes unrecognized by family and friends. What I had not known was that the health issues brought on by childhood abuse share the same qualities that victims experience. They can go unnoticed, become invisible, and often uncontrollable.

Jane Ellen Stevens, in her article "The Adverse Childhood Experiences Study—the Largest Public Health Study You Never Heard Of," discusses the "Flight or Fight Theory" as it pertains to childhood abuse and trauma. Jane is a regular contributor to the Huffington Post, where this article was posted on October 8, 2012.

> The flight, fight, or freeze hormones work really
> well to help us accelerate when we're being chased
> by a vicious dog with big teeth, fight when we're
> cornered, or turn to stone and stop breathing to
> escape detection by a predator. But they become
> toxic when they're turned on for too long.

I was bowled over as I read how the adrenal glands do double time during periods of anxiety and stress. The body is flooded with adrenaline in order to survive the trauma. As a result the brain cannot function effectively in everyday ways such as learning, because the normal messages to the brain are now hindered.

In my early twenties I was diagnosed with an overactive adrenal gland. The doctor prescribed Decadron/dexamethasone for years until my hormones finally balanced out. Never did he or I make a connection of hyperactive adrenal glands with childhood priest abuse and, even if we had, would I have been in touch enough with myself to face the truth of it?

The fact that I wasn't focused on childbearing diminished the concern of very irregular menstrual periods caused by adrenal hyperplasia. I realized how wonderful my body was, considering that it continually found ways to cope. Consciously or unconsciously, my body did what it needed to do to escape from anxiety, anger, depression, fear, and shame.

At last I began to feel and know the connection between my body, mind, and spirit. My body became my prized possession as my understanding of its ability to save me grew. This knowledge sparked anger—an anger I had not really felt before. Finally, I knew the full cost of childhood sex abuse. My disdain for Father Rucker, for the hierarchy of the Church and for all systems that allow pedophiles to rape and harm children knew no bounds. There would be more for me to confront.

34

THE SETTLEMENT

*The good we secure for ourselves is precarious
and uncertain ... until it is secured for all of us
and incorporated into our common life.*

—Jane Addams, *The Subjective Necessity for Social Settlements*

THE PHONE RANG. It was John Manly, my attorney. "Mary, I have good news. The case has settled." It was late November 2006.

"Settled?" I repeated. *After all this time.* "Settled?" I gestured to Mary Ann to listen and pressed the speaker button on the phone.

"Yes," said John. He told us the details of the last few days, how the Archdiocese finally agreed, after stonewalling for months, even years, to settle the cases of forty-five victims whose abuse claims reached back to a period before there was insurance for such situations. "It's good," John said. He was happy to tell us that he had left no money on the table. I had received a generous settlement.

I wanted to reach through the telephone cord and give John a great big hug. Instead I said, "Thank you, John, thank you." I hung up the phone, hugged Mary Ann, and we danced around the kitchen island.

Never had I dreamed of or wanted to press charges. Money was not in my vision until I began to realize, as my case went on, that money mattered to the Catholic Church and was another piece of the equation of secrecy. Realizing this, it became important to me to reach a financial settlement—one that would help make the hierarchy, especially Cardinal Mahony, say "No more." Though money is a poor reason for the church to want to change its ways, it works, and causes the church to see pedophiles as serious liabilities. I wish it were about the safety of children instead. Too often it is not.

It had been a long, hard journey to this point. I paid a price. I will never know the connection between the onset of dystonia and navigating the rough waters of abuse and seeking justice.

All the phone calls and meetings, all the official papers to complete, trips to Los Angeles, the depositions, the disappointment when the criminal case against Father Rucker collapsed, the long slog of anxiety over the progress of the civil cases against Rucker and the church. I felt enormous relief that it was over, and so did John. I was stunned too. After all that time, the realization took a while to sink in. I was actually going to be compensated in tangible ways for a lifetime of challenges. The press did its best to help me with this.

On Saturday, December 2, 2006, the headline in the *Los Angeles Times* headline read, "Archdiocese to Pay $60 Million Over Sex-Abuse Cases." The article mentioned me by name—I think the "former nun" caught people's attention. Another *Los Angeles Times* article the same day by John Spano, "She Can't Forgive Mahony's Inaction," went into detail about my experience of abuse and its impact on my life.

The *Seattle Times* called and sent a reporter and photographer to our house to interview me. The next day my picture was on the front page of the paper. The headline read: 4 Decades after Abuse, Former Nun Faces Past *(Los Angeles Archdiocese) Raped when she was 7 by a Catholic priest, a Bellevue woman—and 44 others who sued the archdiocese in sex-abuse cases—recently reached a $60 million settlement with the church.*

Friends began to call. They were wonderful. "Good for you!" they cheered. "You deserve it." "We are happy for you and wonder, how do you feel today? Relieved? Overwhelmed?" Mostly in that moment, I felt joy. Mary Ann and I kept celebrating the victory. We went out to dinner and toasted each other with champagne. Deserved though it might be, hard-won as it was, it was good fortune and worthy of celebration.

I couldn't help thinking of all the other victims, both those who had received settlements and the many, many others whose suffering was still to be acknowledged. Money alone cannot erase the shame and heal a deeply wounded spirit. Yet settlements are tangible symbols of the church taking responsibility for the damage it has done. As restitution, it can begin to work toward healing.

Money to settle ... Does money settle? Yes, sometimes. It did help me settle. It helped pay my bills. It made it possible for us to take a trip. It helped me to achieve financial stability and it reduced stress and anxiety about the future. But settle completely? Never. I don't think so. It didn't settle once and for all the rough edges and scars of childhood. That kind of settling may take a lifetime. Working through this process of holding the Catholic Church and the abusers within it accountable was a positive experience, though not without emotional cost.

On all fronts, I am better and healed. My mind and spirit are one now. My body and my soul are no longer at war in any way. Shame is a thing of the past. I have settled down. There, I said it. Settled. Perhaps there was a settlement after all, not so much about money, but about me. I hadn't thought about settlement in that way—the way of my being settled in, settled down.

Then my attorney asked if I would like to speak with Cardinal Mahony, and as quickly as that I was unsettled again. The Cardinal had agreed to meet with survivors if they wanted to meet with him.

"Why?"

"It might be helpful as a final piece of closure for you," John said, "and you may have some things you want Mahony to hear."

No way. I am done. I am finished. Not another word given to the church.

Funny thing is, I said yes.

35

INSIDE THE CHAMBER

*...one thing we do know: that man is here for
the sake of other men—above all for those upon
whose smile and well-being our own happiness
depends and also for the countless unknown
souls with whose fate we are connected by a
bond of sympathy.*

—Albert Einstein, *Living Philosophies*

WE MET AT the Los Angeles Courthouse in the Chamber of Charles McCoy, Superior Court Judge, at 9:30 a.m. on December 14, 2006. This was my time and I felt it. I brought my promise with me, that wherever I am, I will show up as love. That was the intention I held. I was going to have time with Cardinal Mahony, a man whose name I had heard and seen in the news repeatedly over the past four years. I only had to show up, tell the truth, pay attention to what had heart and meaning, and not be attached to the outcome—words I have lived and cherished from anthropologist Angeles Arrien.

Mary Ann and I rode with my attorneys to the courthouse. No red convertible that day, either. My attorneys did not go into the judge's chamber with us. Attorneys for both sides agreed that they would stay out of these conversations between victims/ survivors and Cardinal Mahony.

It was time. Mary Ann and I were summoned into the judge's chambers to meet Cardinal Mahony and Judge McCoy. My eyes swept across the chamber room, taking in as much as I could of the environment, maybe to have power over it. I liked it. It was rather warm and friendly. Maybe it was the children's portraits on the bookcase that helped me feel comfortable. Oh yes, and the sun streaming in the window and the kind face of Judge McCoy. And then there was the Cardinal in his black robe with a cross and that beautiful magenta cap on his head. A strange getup, if you haven't grown up Catholic. Not so welcoming.

A circle of furniture—a couch, the judge's chair, three wooden armchairs, and an upholstered chair arranged around an oval coffee table. Circles. Circles. Circles. The circle of the rosary I loved to pray. The circle of myself, spinning round and round, would stop here. Had I come full circle from the Women's Circle fourteen years ago? Then I was just beginning to awaken to my memories. Now I knew and understood so much more about who I was.

Judge McCoy invited Mary Ann and me to sit anywhere other than in his chair or the upholstered chair where the Cardinal sat. Judge McCoy sat at the far left of the circle directly across from Cardinal Mahony. Mary Ann sat across from me with empty chairs on either side of her. I chose the end of the couch—as close as possible to the soft chair where the Cardinal was seated. I wanted very much to look into his eyes to see what was there. I wanted to feel as if no one else were in the room, or listening to us, in order to speak the truth with ease. The truth. No more lies. No more hiding. No more shame.

And so we began.

Judge McCoy was the first to break the stillness in the chamber. He gave some background as to how these sessions came about. Cardinal Mahony thanked me for coming all the way from Seattle. He said, "This is your time, you can say anything you want to say to me and ask me any question."

I turned and leaned my body toward him. The judge faded away. Mary Ann faded away. Cardinal Mahony and I were alone. I looked into his eyes and said, "The first thing it seems I need to do is cry." I was overwhelmed with emotion and so for a few moments, I wept. Maybe it was like facing Archbishop Thomas Murphy to confront him after he fired me for choosing to live out my life from a place of truth and love. Maybe it was awareness that there was no turning back. My life in the church was over and this was the last stop. Really. The tears, I believe, were about release.

Facing the church and a priest for the last time, I was no longer a child.

I began to speak "Cardinal Mahony, we are about the same age and have lived a long time."

He said, "I am seventy."

I said, "I am sixty-six. And I want to tell you my story."

I was not sure how much the Cardinal really knew about me. I wanted Cardinal Mahony to know my story. It was important to me to be seen. I brought Little Mary to speak about how Father Rucker hurt her. I wanted her to reclaim the voice she lost so long ago, to give her a chance to say what it meant for her to be raped by a priest that she trusted and saw every day for five years.

And so I told my story, as the Cardinal listened. I told him everything, not shying away from the details of the sexual violence I suffered, not leaving out any piece of its impact on my life, my life in the church and out of it.

"That, Cardinal Mahony," I summarized, "is a simple version of a very painful part of my journey. At some level, I really believed that if I let this abuse surface, I would have to leave the church I loved and all that I knew to be my life and my way in the world. And that is exactly what has happened."

Cardinal Mahony said, "Mary, I am so, so very sorry for what has happened to you and for what the church has done."

"Thank you," I said. "I've thought a lot about confession, reconciliation, and forgiveness. I don't think it is very easy to forgive and yet, in another sense, it is. I've thought hard and long about confession. What I learned in Catholic school as a child was that the first thing I must do to be forgiven is to tell the truth about my sin, then look at all the ways I might right the wrong and make amends for my sin and mend the brokenness I have caused. I must tell the person I am sorry and hope for forgiveness.

"Cardinal Mahony, you cannot restore my childhood, but you can make my situation and that of the other 556 victims better by settling with those who want a settlement and by making amends, saying you are sorry, and asking forgiveness. You must find ways. If it means selling the Catholic Church's oil wells, parking lots, restaurants, and properties, you must do that and be the leader you are called to be.

"You are a man of power, Cardinal Mahony. You must use your power for good and be the shepherd the church needs. I imagine it is difficult to be in your shoes, where religion and politics and the law come together. It's nearly impossible.

"I wonder what Jesus would do if he were in your shoes today.

"I imagine you may feel boxed in because, if you were to tell the truth about everything you know, you may be implicated or indicted."

Cardinal Mahony raised his hand. "I really don't feel boxed in."

I continued. "Please do not stand in the way of justice by protecting the church at the expense of children. You must settle up quickly with victims. Since 2001, I have poured psychic, emotional, and spiritual energy into this process, as many victims have, and the longer the church stalls, with appeals and appeals, justice cannot prevail and victims cannot heal. Abuse is heaped upon abuse. You can do something about this."

Cardinal Mahony answered, "Believe me, Mary, we are in the process of looking at our assets and we will sell and it will hurt, but not nearly as much as it has hurt the victims. We are working hard with the insurance companies and this is taking more time and effort than we expected or than victims deserve."

Cardinal Mahony shared about the new policies and procedures in place for children's safety—the zero-tolerance policy established in the early 2000s. He also said that when that policy was established, he could have and should have removed six priests—he named them—known pedophiles, still in ministry. He said, "Looking back, I could have removed them. I should have and I didn't. I'm sorry."

Judge McCoy stepped in to explain the court cases pending and how the California constitution protects privacy. He said that while he may read some of the records on priests and be appalled, he must, by law, protect their right to privacy, "or I might as well take off my robes."

I moved on to the point about the church's rewarding priests who have harbored pedophile priests, such as Bishop Skylstad of Spokane, who was removed from his position when it was discovered that he knowingly allowed priests to abuse boys in the very rectory in which he lived. Then he was appointed chair of the United States Conference of Catholic Bishos. Also, Cardinal Law, whom the people of Boston rose up against and said, "We don't want you as our leader. You have not been the leader you are called to be." He was ousted, only to land a position at the Vatican and be asked to celebrate a mass for our late Holy Father, Pope John Paul II. These awards to negligent priests made no sense to me.

Cardinal Mahony responded, "Yes, I agree with you, Mary. Did you know that no American Bishop went to that mass celebrated by Cardinal Law?"

"No, I had not known that," I said.

Cardinal Mahony added, "I was shocked to find, upon becoming Cardinal in Los Angeles and getting familiar with Father Rucker's records, that he was still a pastor."

I asked Cardinal Mahony at that point, "If you know of a priest who has committed a crime of sex abuse against one child, would you have the authorities bring the priest to justice?"

"Absolutely," he answered.

"We are all as sick as our secrets," I said, "and an organization is as sick as its secrets. The church must bring this dark chapter into the light. It is a systemic problem. You can use your power to help move this work of healing and mending along. Look at your options and choose the way of Jesus, the Good Shepherd."

Cardinal Mahony said, "You know, in the early days, we really thought that if a person got good therapeutic treatment, he could be reinstalled into a limited ministry. That was the best thinking of experts at the time."

"It doesn't take an expert or higher education to know that you don't mess with a little child," I said. "You know the scripture better than I, but what is that passage—'It is better for him to have...'"

Cardinal Mahony continued "...a millstone fastened around his neck and be cast into the sea..."

And I finished the passage, "...than to bring scandal to a little child."

In that moment I knew we were on the same page.

"I know I need to forgive you," I said. "I need to forgive Father Rucker. I need to forgive the church, and I will. I will do my work to make forgiveness complete and you must help by telling the truth, or you prevent all of us from completing this sacrament of reconciliation."

I paused, thinking of one more thing that was very much needed.

"Father Rucker must tell the truth."

"Thank you, Mary," he said, "I am so sorry for how the church has hurt you. I am very, very sorry."

"Thank you," I said.

A multitude of tears spilled in and out of this conversation. I put my head down for a moment to listen to my heart for anything left unsaid and, from deep within, came the words.

"Now I want to speak about being gay.

"I never finished my story about my work in the Chancery Department in Seattle, Cardinal Mahony. After three years there,

I came out in the workplace. I believe I had to tell the truth about Father Rucker before I could tell the next truth about my life. One truth leads to another and another and another. I was naive about coming out to the church. I thought everyone would be happy for me. Some of my colleagues were, and some were confused and didn't know what to say. I was fired from my position by Archbishop Thomas Murphy for my choice to live out my life and so ended my thirty-four year career in Catholic education and ministry. Again, Cardinal Mahony, I felt abused, and again the messages of the church were conflicted. God loves me as I am. God's joy is seeing me fully alive. Being gay is God's mystery. Why can we not live in the mystery? Must we always have the answers?"

I challenged Cardinal Mahony to revisit the last letter written by Cardinal Ratzinger on homosexuality. I said, "It is a terrible letter, saying homosexuality is inordinate and unnatural." I begged the Cardinal to open his eyes and see my situation in a new light.

The Cardinal was happy to report to me that the College of Bishops had just approved a new policy on Pastoral Care of Homosexuals.

My insides began to revolt. *He does not get it.* I responded, "I don't want pastoral care. I don't need pastoral care. I want full inclusion and participation in the church. I want to be a leader in the church. It is my birthright, my baptismal right. I want to take my partner to church, if not to be married, then to have a commitment ceremony and celebration of our love. I want the same resources and support other couples are entitled to receive."

I could tell by his eyes that I had been heard and listened to in this moment and this conversation.

We paused. I cried tears stored from the past. I cried for the treatment of lesbians and gays. I cried for the youth who have no place in the church and are homeless and on the streets. I cried for all the gay persons who have taken their lives because the church had not found them good enough. The shame about being gay was a heavy burden that I needed to release. It was released completely that day.

The Cardinal ended by saying he would place my name on a three-by-five card and add it to his personal chapel altar, along with the names of the other thirty survivors he'd spoken with and the cancer patients he keeps in his prayers, and pray daily for me.

I wasn't sure how I felt about that. Something inside me didn't want to be prayed for and something did. I wanted action and change, justice and resolution for the many persons harmed by the church. And yet, I said, "Thank you for that and please take action to mend the broken places and settle with victims."

Silence fell over the room. We were finished.

We looked at each other. The end had come. We all stood. I went to Cardinal Mahony. We started to shake hands, but hugged instead. Two human beings connected, if only for a brief moment.

Little Mary had her say; grown-up gay Mary had her say. I wondered if the others changed in any way. Was Cardinal Mahony different from an hour and a half ago? More settled? More just? More determined to make things right? I don't know. Was this just another formality for him? Did he leave the whole issue of priest abuse in the judge's chambers, or did he leave with a desire to right his wrongs and the wrongs inflicted by some priests on their prey—vulnerable children? What I do know is that I had changed.

36

FINALLY FORGIVENESS

*The more we love, the more capacity we have
for forgiveness. Love and forgiveness go
together. Without love there is no forgiveness.
Without forgiveness there is little love.*

—Mary Dispenza

I HAVE ASKED MYSELF so many times, "What is forgiveness?" Is
forgiving another really necessary for healing? The answer hasn't
come easily. As I dissociated myself from my history of abuse,
I lived in a state of make-believe, thinking everything was just
fine, even my ability to forgive. Daniel Mackler, a therapist in
New York State, has said:

"People who are dissociated feel they have mastered forgiveness. But this is only because they completely deny the harm
done to them—and the damage remaining. The enlightened
forgive spontaneously and without effort because they have fully
embraced their damaged parts and grieved every honest ounce
of their misery."

The healthier I became, the more I began to deconstruct the
concept of forgiveness for myself. I wasn't sure I wanted to forgive
Father Rucker—or needed to forgive him.

When I was a child in Catholic school, I was taught that if a
person said, "I'm sorry," then I needed to forgive. The nuns never
told me what forgiveness might look like or feel like. All I knew
about forgiveness was that God forgave me and that good and
loving people forgive also. As a child I wanted to forgive as Jesus

and the good folks did. Still, it seemed easier as a kid to say, "I'm sorry" than to say "I forgive you."

Father Rucker said he was sorry at the end of our meeting in 1992, the time we met face-to-face for the first time. Father Rucker asked for forgiveness, yet he continued to molest other victims after saying those words to me. This is a mystery, not mine to solve. On that day, my response was, "I want to forgive you. I will forgive you. It will take some time."

It did take time as I uncovered layer after layer about my childhood and the crimes of Father Rucker. Like peeling away the prickly leaves of an artichoke, I finally found my heart of forgiveness when I realized that I had a choice. I could hold on to grievances toward Father Rucker and the Catholic Church, or let them go. Ultimately, though, I came to understand that forgiveness meant more than letting go of grievances. It meant letting go of a burden that held me captive.

A Zen story tells of two monks meeting a woman who needed help crossing the river. One monk carried the woman across on his shoulders and then put her down. The two monks went on their way. Time passed and the other monk, a brooding, preoccupied man, spoke out, "Brother, you should not have carried the woman across the river. Our holy rule teaches that we must avoid contact with women." The second monk responded, "Brother, I set her down on the side of the river, while you are still carrying her."

This story drove home to me that holding on to a big hurt is like carrying a heavy, heavy bag of trash all day, every day, even into night. Like the first monk, I wanted to put all this down at the side of the river and cross over to a new day.

The words of Thich Nhat Hanh are a reminder that I must empty in order to fill up with peace.

...I transform the garbage in myself

So you will not have to suffer.

We are in the world

To bring peace and joy to each other.

Forgiving Father Rucker was critical to living a full and healthy life. I had to let go. Give it over—give it up, the fire, the anger, the hurt, the shame. Give it to the universe to transform. Give it to God to lift up. It was not good for my health. The weight of it all still affected me in negative ways that limited my creative energy, intimacy, and love.

I decided I would face Father Rucker for the last time and say—and really mean it—"I forgive you."

37

UNSPLIT

Your journey has molded you for your greater good and it was exactly what it needed to be. Don't think you've lost time. There is no shortcutting to life. It took each and every situation you have encountered to bring you to the now. And now is right on time.

—Asha Tyson, writer, public speaker

IT WAS A blue-gray day in Los Angeles. That familiar thick cloud of smog settled over the city in a way that speaks home to me. I was visiting my family. This was the day—the day I would say, "I forgive you" and really mean it.

I didn't mention to anyone where I was going as I took off that morning to the Nazareth House, a Catholic residential community operated by the Sisters of Nazareth. *How fitting,* I thought, *that it sits nestled on Manning Avenue, a street named after Cardinal Manning—a name I remember from my childhood.*

The Nazareth House was Father Rucker's home since 2002. I started out early that morning counting on the Los Angeles Freeway to raise my blood pressure a few points. The morning traffic was as frenetic as ever. Cars whizzed by me on my right and on my left.

Finally after about forty-five minutes of intense driving, I saw the Manning Avenue exit. I made a couple of turns and my faithful driving companion, Siri, said, "You have reached your destination."

"Now what?" I asked myself.

I got out of my car, took a snapshot of the rather drab entrance, noticed the white, marble-like statue of our blessed mother, and began to pray a familiar prayer: "Hail Mary full of grace, the Lord is with you … " I asked wisdom to know what to do now. I knew why I was there. It was about forgiveness for the last time.

I went in. There was a desk and sign-in counter. An elderly sister dressed in her full habit, was sitting on top of the desk chatting with the helper behind it. The sister had a girlish attitude and sassy air about her. My hunch was that she was in her late seventies. Neither paid much attention to me.

I approached the desk and asked, "May I speak to someone about the Nazareth House?" I was directed down the hallway to the admissions office. I asked for a brochure. I wandered down the hallway to the chapel. I was drawn to the gilded gold-framed picture of Our Lady of Perpetual Help, mother of my childhood. Many Tuesday evenings in high school I would pick up my girl friends in the lavender Chevrolet and drive to our Lady of Perpetual Help Devotions at St. Alphonsus Church. I began to pray: "Oh Mother of Perpetual Help, my heart is full of confidence in thee on account of thy name. I have come to ask your maternal help in all my miseries. Oh, deign to hearken to me from the heights of Heaven but come to my help, oh loving Mother …"

Tears began to flow. *I am alone with God. I am home with God.*

As I walked back down the hallway I noticed a sister working at a computer. I stood at the door of her small office.

"Excuse me, Sister. May I come in?"

She turned from her computer and said, "Yes, do." I introduced myself. She took off her glasses and covered one eye with her hand in order to protect it from the glare of the overhead light and sun.

"I'm Sister Bernadette."

I began to stumble and fumble, searching for words not rehearsed.

"I … I'm not really sure why I am here, Sister. Bernadette." I mentioned Father Rucker.

Sister Bernadette quickly corrected me. "He is not a priest."

"I know." And yet, I continued to talk as if he were.

Sister Bernadette covered her ears. "I am not supposed to hear this. I'm not supposed to talk about this."

"Oh I am sorry, Sister."

"He is not here," she muttered softly.

I moved on. Not wanting to offend Sister Bernadette, I broached the subject of forgiveness. This was a topic with which she was much more at home. As I talked it became clearer and clearer to me that I didn't need, nor want, to see Father Rucker. I knew Father Rucker believed he was forgiven. There really was no reason to tell him again. Coming to the Nazareth Home was about me. It was there that I finished my story and brought it to completion.

A silence filled the small office. It seemed brighter now than when I entered. The sun was casting beams of light through the space we shared.

"He is not here," she said for the second time. "Perhaps that is your answer."

This time I heard the words and accepted them as gift. Father Rucker was gone. It really seemed that way. I said in a resolved voice—

"That is my answer, Sister."

"Lovely," she replied.

We smiled. She nodded. I rose and left.

* * *

Walking toward my car, I whispered, "Father Rucker, wherever you are, I forgive you."

That day I gave myself a great and lasting gift. I let go. Really. Unreservedly. Completely.

Forgiveness has a way of opening us up to love and healing. It cracks us open so we can be so much more than we ever were for others and ourselves.

Marianne Williamson, among my favorite spiritual writers says, "The practice of forgiveness is our most important contribution to the healing of the world."

Truly, grace, love, and forgiveness have healed me, making love and intimacy possible. I knew love, not intimacy. The human spirit craves both. It wasn't enough for me to hear "I love you" from family and friends. I needed to feel it, smell it, touch and be touched by it. Now I have both.

It is my time to give hope, love, and support to those on their journey of healing from childhood abuse to health and wholeness. The call inspires me and gives my life renewed meaning and purpose.

In the summer of 2013 I took my place on the stage at the Town Hall in Seattle. I brought together four expert panelists to join Michael D'Antonio in discussing his book, *Mortal Sins: Sex, Crime, and the Era of Catholic Scandal.* I was one of the panelists and had never thought of myself as an expert on this topic. As I see it, an expert on a topic or subject is someone who has given a zillion hours to a particular field of study or life. In that sense perhaps I was an expert—at least an expert witness to the truth and story of one survivor/victim of childhood priest abuse and the power and ability to heal and hope for a renewed Catholic Church, placing children's safety above protecting its priests.

I scanned the audience. Strangers, victims/survivors of priest abuse, friends, and colleagues were there—eager to learn and understand.

Each of the panelists shared from his or her perspective and life. In a flash it was Q and A time. We shared answers. The evening ended with applause of gratitude. Some people thanked me for the gift of my story and hope for the future. Slowly one by one the hall emptied. I took advantage of a moment to use the bathroom.

I leaned over the sink, washed my hands, stood up straight and unabashed. I leaned in to the mirror and whispered,

"Dear God, tonight I am UNSPLIT."

I flashed myself a smile and the same warm familiar dimple appeared. Little Mary was smiling back at me.

Mary Dispenza

Afterword

George Neville Rucker

Mr. Rucker is ranked in *BishopAccountability.org* as number one on a list of the ten top abusive priests in the Los Angeles Archdiocese. Yet he has never served a day in jail.

Cardinal Mahony

Cardinal Mahony is retired. The current archbishop of Los Angeles, Jose Gomez, announced January 31, 2013, that the cardinal would "no longer have any administrative or public duties" in the Archdiocese. This action followed revelations in documents related to the 2007 settlement that were released on the same day, revelations about the church's cover-up and actions designed to protect the church rather than minister to its victims. Gomez called these revelations "brutal and painful reading," in a letter sent to every parish in the Archdiocese.

The U.S. Catholic Bishops and Child Sex Crimes

Many bishops are culpable of concealing evidence and passing on priest predators from parish to parish. In spite of this crime, they still have their jobs or have been promoted.

The Mishandling of Child Sex Abuse by the Roman Catholic Church

The Dallas Morning News did a yearlong investigation after the 2002 revelation that cases of abuse were widespread in the church. The results, made public in 2004, showed that even after the public outcry, priests were moved out of the countries where they had been accused and were still in contact with children, despite church claims to the contrary. ("Runaway Priests Hiding in Plain Sight: Untouchable," June 20, 2004.)

At the time of the biggest settlement ever in the Catholic Church of Los Angeles in 2006, the attorneys for the survivors and the Archdiocese of Los Angeles agreed that the records of the perpetrators would also be released. It took until 2013 for this to happen and still the records were incomplete.

Pope Francis's Response to Priest Abuse

Pope Francis has been a breath of fresh air with his focus on the poor and positive interactions with the public and the media. Yet for the first nine months of his tenure in office, Francis gave little public attention to the scandals of priest sexual abuse of children and the institutional cover-up. In a PEW Research poll taken in March 2013, seventy percent of Catholics surveyed ranked "Addressing the priest abuse scandal" as the top priority for Pope Francis. Still, when Francis outlined his top three goals for his bishops, addressing clergy abuse was not among them. Pope Francis has taken some steps in the right direction by forming a commission to advise him in ways to keep children safe and hold bishops accountable for protecting priest who prey on children. The October 6, 2014 editorial of the *National Catholic Reporter* states that the actions of Pope Francis are finally showing progress since laicizing Archbishop Josef Wesolowski who was found guilty of sexually molesting minors. Josef Wesolowski is allegedly under house arrest in the Vatican City. This is progress. There remains much more to be done. Children continue to be molested today.

SNAP—Survivors Network of Those Abused by Priests

Barbara Blaine founded SNAP in 1988. Today Barbara Blaine and David Clohessy serve as directors. SNAP works tirelessly to achieve two goals: to heal the wounded and to protect the vulnerable. The organization has more than 12,000 members in fifty-six countries and support groups meet in over sixty cities across the U.S. and the world.

On September 13, 2013, leaders of SNAP, joined by attorneys from the Center for Constitutional Rights, filed an eighty-four-page complaint with the United Nations Committee on the Rights of the Child, detailing how Vatican officials tolerate and enable the systematic and widespread concealing of rape and child sex crimes. The outcome was not good news for the Vatican. They received a scathing report from the U.N. committee concluding, "Vatican officials failed to report sex abuse charges properly, had moved priests rather than discipline them, and had failed to pay adequate compensation to victims. Although the panel did not explicitly say that the Holy See had violated any of its obligations under the anti-torture treaty, which it ratified in 2002, panel members said that was implicit in the criticism." ("UN Panel Slams Vatican on Priest Abuse," Huffington Post, Nicole Winfield, May 23, 2014)

Detective James Brown

James Brown retired after completing over thirty-three years with the Los Angeles Police Department. During the last twenty-five years of his career with the LAPD, Brown was assigned to the department's Juvenile Division. These years were dedicated to the investigation and supervision of child abuse and child exploitation cases and Internet crimes against children.

Presently, he is an instructor of criminal justice at Volunteer State Community College in Tennessee. The investigation of Father Rucker is discussed every semester as an example of a preferential sexual predator who victimized innocent children.

John Manly

John Manly was selected as California Super Lawyer for 2014. This distinction is awarded to no more than five percent of attorneys in the state. Super lawyers are determined by using a rigorous selection process involving peer nominations and evaluations. John continues to work tirelessly to keep children and youth safe. John is senior attorney and founding partner at Manly, Stewart and Finaldi.

The Statutes of Limitation

It is fact that it often takes years or decades for a victim of child sexual abuse—especially by a priest—to grasp what has happened to them. It is right and just that the opportunity to seek justice be just as long. The crime is predicated on shame, secrecy, and power. While work is being done to make statutes of limitations longer or abolish them completely in civil cases, the Catholic Church has successfully halted such proposals in many states.

The Religious of the Sacred Heart of Mary

The sisters known as the Religious of the Sacred Heart of Mary serve in thirteen countries in diverse ministries. They are "ordinary people with an extraordinary calling—to live generously in the love of Jesus, finding the face of God in the beauty and the anguish of this fragile world" (www.rshm.org). The sisters of the Western Province are focusing their energy and service on the ever-increasing problem of the trafficking of young girls and women.

Mary and Mary Ann

Marriage between same-sex couples became legal in the state of Washington with the passage of Referendum 74 on November 6, 2012. After a very long engagement, Mary married Mary Ann on February 10, 2013 and the children, Alli, Logan, Rita, Kurt, Jamie, and Tess, leapt and shouted for joy as they tossed yellow rose petals into the air.

And the children shout HOORAY!

Acknowledgments

Friends will do all kinds of things for you.

—A. Lamorisse, *The Red Balloon*

YES, MY NAME is on the cover as the author, and that I am. Truth is there could be a subset of names beneath mine of family and friends who in one way or another are here in this story—in the living, loving, and the writing of it. You are the reasons I could write. At the top of this list is my spouse and my love, Mary Ann, whose beauty and love sustain me. I thank my witnesses who listened to bits and pieces of my manuscript along the way—the ones who nodded their heads in affirmation as I read to them and the ones who helped me go deeper by seeking understanding and clarity. I thank my cheerleaders Christina Baldwin who loved me through the pages, helped me get started, and inspired me to keep going, and Sharlene Martin for believing in me and reminding me that the world needs this story. I applaud the first of my editors, Chuck Sambuchino and Chris Megargee, who saw the potential in *SPLIT* and helped me develop the story. Thanks to Anthony Flacco for additional editing, and to Leah Tracosas Jenness for finishing touches. Special thanks to my dear friend, writer and proofreader Nancy Bartlett, and to Kathy Campbell for setup and design. Thanks to the diligent readers who questioned this and that with attention and sensitivity. Thank you, brave survivors of sexual abuse for your stories—the greatest gift we have to give each other—and to SNAP for endless work in protecting children. A final thank you to everyone who reads *SPLIT* and sees the possibility for forgiveness, hope, and the power to heal the broken places in our lives and the Catholic Church. This story is for all of us.

ation can be obtained at www.ICGtesting.com
SA
80815
0005B/151/P